Cooking with Coconut Oil

<u>Page</u>
76

Bacon Sweet potato
Meatballs

cooking with

COCONUT OIL

Gluten-Free, Grain-Free Recipes for *good living*

Elizabeth Nyland

The Countryman Press
Woodstock, VT
www.countrymanpress.com

Published by The Countryman Press, P.O. Box 748, Woodstock, VT 05091
Distributed by W. W. Norton & Company, Inc., 500 Fifth Avenue, New York, NY 10110

Printed in the United States

Cooking with Coconut Oil
ISBN 978-1-58157-236-0

10 9 8 7 6 5 4 3 2 1

To Adrian, Cohen, and Isla.

Without your undying support, unmatched
taste-testing abilities, and willingness to try
any weird combos I could think of,
this book would never have happened.

I thank you all from the bottom of my heart.

Contents

Preface

My website, GuiltyKitchen.com, has been around since the summer after my first child was born. As a newly minted stay-at-home mom, I found that I needed something to expend my creative energy on that wasn't a wriggling, screaming baby or a constantly hungry toddler. I had been a trained chef and had worked in the food industry for about ten years, so I knew I could come up with new recipes for eternity if I needed to. Plus, it had been my dream to write a cookbook since I was a very little girl in my mother's kitchen.

When I started my blog, I didn't know how to take or edit a good picture, how to write a blog post, or even how I was supposed to get people to find my site and read it! Over the course of three years, I went from a standard-issue food blog to a health blog. I did raw food, vegetarian food, completely guilty food. But then, through years of experimentation, I settled on a way of eating that made me feel so amazing, I could never consider eating any other way.

We rented a house in a little neighborhood on the Saanich Peninsula on the South End of Vancouver Island. We raised chickens, grew our own fruits and vegetables, and reveled in our ability to grow our own food, but we struggled to find a way of eating that everyone in the family enjoyed and thrived on. One day we met our neighbors. They were "Paleo."

Huh? What's Paleo? I asked a lot of questions about it, we had dinner together, we shared tips and recipes, and they lent me a few recipe books I could try. All the trendy "diets" I'd ever read about—no processed food, gluten-free, dairy-free, grain-free—they were all rolled into this one "diet."

I fell in love with this style of eating. I ate what I loved the most: grass-fed or pastured meats, wild-caught fish and seafood, fresh fruits and vegetables, eggs, nuts and seeds, and healthy fats such as coconut, avocado, and extra-virgin olive oil. I began experimenting with various flours, fats, spices, nuts, fruits, meats, and other tasty things. In my recipes for baked goods, I substituted coconut flour and other gluten-free flours. These ingredients added nutrients, protein, and fiber. Who knew desserts could actually be healthy for you?

The fact that fats are good for you was a turning point in my relationship with food, and coconut oil is one that kept appearing in recipe after recipe. Saturated fats could be good for you?! I was flabbergasted. I spent hours researching scientific articles and then just started making recipes, my favorite way to experiment: on myself.

Coconut oil is a lovely addition to any kind of recipe, from savory to sweet, as it is a bit of a nutritional chameleon. With its slight tropical scent and creamy consistency, coconut oil has become the most used ingredient in my pantry. Because it is semi-hard at room temperature it makes a great replacement for butter in baking but is also quite useful in salad dressings, frying, and general cookery. All the recipes in this book are technically Paleo, but they are also all-around healthy dishes that anyone, on any diet, will love.

My health (and that of my family) and also my passion for cooking have been completely renewed with this new lifestyle and I hope you will feel the same way once you try my recipes.

ELIZABETH NYLAND

P.S. Just in case you want to try it, here are some more specifics about the Paleo diet:

With an emphasis on whole, unprocessed foods, the Paleo diet (or lifestyle, as I like to put it) is based on eating the most nutritionally dense foods, while avoiding those foods that promote inflammation, hormone imbalances, or chronic disease. With that in mind, we avoid dairy, refined sugar, grains (including corn), legumes (including peanuts and soy), refined vegetable oils, and processed foods.

So what is allowed?

Grass-fed or pastured meats (beef, pork, chicken, lamb, game meats, etc.), wild-caught fish and seafood, fresh fruits and vegetables, eggs, nuts and seeds, and healthy fats such as coconut, avocado, and extra-virgin olive oil.

The Health Benefits of Coconut Oil

- Filled with lauric acid (boosts immune function and heart health)
- Contains high levels of **medium-chain triglycerides** (MCTs) shown to help burn abdominal fat
- Rich in polyphenols (an antioxidant)
- Helps fight wrinkles, sagging skin, and age spots by warding off free radicals that cause premature aging and degenerative diseases
- Shown to lower bad cholesterol
- Helps boost thyroid function, which can lead to weight loss
- Helps control blood sugar levels and improves insulin secretion
- Contains antimicrobial lipids, capric acid, and caprylic acid, which have antifungal, antibacterial, and antiviral properties
- Helps humans absorb more nutrients during digestion
- MCT oils are easily converted into fuel used by brain cells for improved brain function and have been shown to have therapeutic effects on several brain disorders, mainly Alzheimer's and other neurological disorders

- Increases energy and endurance by providing a quick source of energy
- from the MCTs
- Reduces inflammation
- Dramatically reduces rate of seizures in epileptic children

ADDITIONAL BENEFITS OF COCONUT OIL

- Helps in the healthy growth of hair, and aids in the control of dandruff.
- Great as a conditioner
- Makes an excellent skin conditioner on all skin types, especially dry skin
- Helps relieve dry, itchy skin
- Speeds up wound healing
- Can help fight infections because of its antifungal, antiviral, and antibacterial properties.
- Reduces symptoms of psoriasis, eczema, dermatitis, and other skin issues
- Has been shown to block about 20 percent of the sun's harmful UV rays
- Has been used as mouthwash in India (called oil pulling) for centuries

COCONUT FLOUR BENEFITS

- Gluten-free
- High-fiber
- High-protein
- Low in net carbohydrates (most of the carbs come from the fiber)
- Low glycemic index (great for diabetics)

About the Ingredients

Some of the ingredients in *Cooking with Coconut Oil* might not seem familiar to you, but with a little careful exploration of your local grocer, health-food store, or specialty shops, you should be able to find every ingredient.

AGED BALSAMIC VINEGAR

Traditional Balsamic Vinegar of Modena and Balsamic Vinegar of Modena are two different substances. The former is the real deal, even being protected by the European Union's Protected Designation of Origin. Traditional balsamic vinegar is aged for a minimum of twelve years and is made from a reduction of pressed grapes. They go through a succession of different wooden barrels (each becoming smaller as the years go on). The resulting thick vinegar is sweet and sour with notes of wood and grape, and is equally delicious drizzled over ice cream as it is mixed into dressings. The latter is thin, very vinegary, and best left to be used in salad dressing only. You can find aged balsamic vinegar at any fine food shop.

APPLE CIDER VINEGAR

Raw, unfiltered apple cider vinegar is made from apple juice that is fermented into hard apple cider, then fermented a second time to apple cider vinegar. The healthiest versions will say "contains the mother" on the label. The mother is a colony of beneficial bacteria that forms in the vinegar during fermentation. Apple cider vinegar not only tastes great in recipes, and helps create a leavening effect (when combined with baking soda) in some of the baking recipes in this book, but it also has almost unlimited health benefits. It's good for everything—it can be used as a face toner, as an acid reflux and heartburn remedy, for lowering blood pressure, for relieving bug bites

and sunburns, as hair conditioner, as aftershave, and as a weight loss aid. I add it to my water every day for a little extra flavor.

COCONUT AMINOS

Coconut aminos are made from the raw sap of the coconut tree that is exuded from the flowering blossoms (which will eventually turn into coconuts). It is naturally aged or sun dried and is usually blended with sea salt. Coconut aminos are a soy-free alternative to soy sauce and contain much less sodium as well. If you cannot find coconut aminos, a wheat-free, gluten-free soy sauce (known as tamari) will do.

COCONUT BUTTER

Coconut butter, also known as coconut manna, coconut spread, coconut cream concentrate, and creamed coconut, is the dried whole flesh (both the meat and the oil) of the coconut that has been pureed into a dense, smooth, nutritious spread. You can make your own by putting a minimum of 4 cups of dried, unsweetened coconut flakes or shreds into a food processor for 15 to 20 minutes until extremely smooth. Coconut butter is perfect in baking, in sauces, as a topping, and eaten straight out of the jar!

COCONUT CREAM

Coconut cream is the thick white cream that floats to the top of a can of coconut milk (if you don't shake it). It is also available as a standalone product. Coconut milk is usually 53 to 55 percent coconut extract, and coconut cream is much higher, usually 70 percent or more. Both are made from the grated flesh of mature brown coconuts; the only main difference is more water is added to coconut milk. Look for cans of coconut milk that have no stabilizers (guar gum) added or simply refrigerate a can for 4 hours or more and scoop the cream from the top. Drink the water that is left in the bottom or use in smoothies.

COCONUT OIL: VIRGIN, RAW, ORGANIC, COLD-PRESSED, REFINED?

What kind of coconut oil should you buy? In this book, all the recipes were made with organic, cold-pressed, unrefined coconut oil. For the most health benefits, always choose unrefined, "virgin" coconut oil, preferably from organic sources and either "expeller-" or "cold-pressed." Refined coconut oils can be treated with various chemicals and processed using very high heats, thus compromising all the health benefits we've talked about. The color should be white and the ingredient list should read "100 percent coconut oil" and nothing else. The flavor will be mild and almost sweet with a slight hint of coconuts.

PASTURED EGGS

Pastured eggs are the eggs from laying hens who have been allowed to roam free with unlimited access to the outdoors. They eat grass, bugs, plants, greens, and vegetable trimmings and are usually supplemented with grain-based feeds. Because there is no regulation behind the use of the terms "free run" or "free range," it is best to find pastured eggs by speaking with neighboring farmers, visiting local farmers' markets, or asking your grocer about the eggs sold in your grocery store.

SWEET POTATOES OR YAMS?

Sweet potatoes are a starchy tuberous root. They come in many variations, from orange to yellow, purple, red, brown, pink, and even beige. Sweet potatoes are not yams. Yams are a completely different species of starchy tubers grown mainly in Africa, Asia, Latin America, and the Caribbean and are a very important food staple. Yams can grow up to almost five feet long and weigh up to 150 pounds or more! Because of the confusion, most labeling in the US is required to state either "yam" or "sweet potato." This book, when calling for sweet potatoes, refers to the orange-flesh variety.

Breakfast

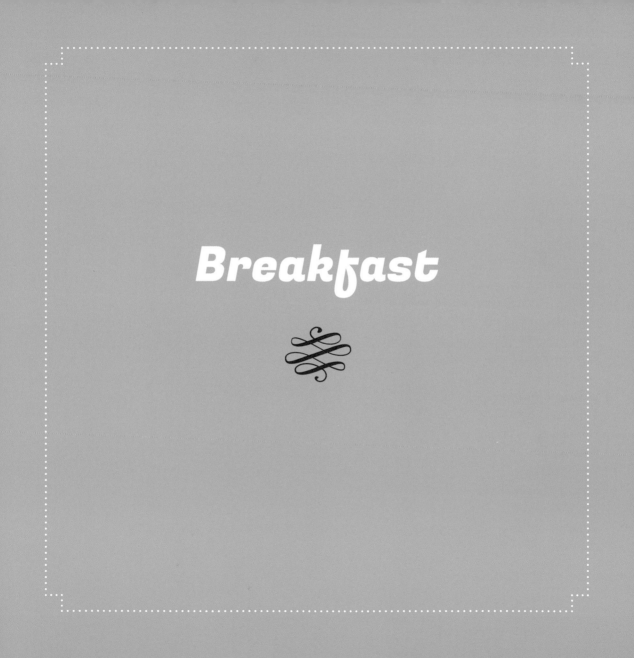

Coconut Pancakes

Pancakes are a favorite breakfast food for our kids. When we gave up grains, there was a period of time when we just didn't know what to make for breakfast and snacks. Creativity flourished, though, and many pancake recipes were born. This one is the best of them all. Not only are they great fresh out of the pan, served any way you would normally have pancakes, but they freeze well and can be reheated in the toaster or eaten cold out of hand.

YIELD: 18 PANCAKES

¼ cup coconut oil, melted

¼ cup nut butter (such as almond, cashew, or macadamia)

2 tbsp honey or maple syrup (optional)

4 pastured eggs

1 tbsp pure vanilla extract

½ tsp apple cider vinegar

3 tbsp coconut flour

½ tsp ground cinnamon

¼ tsp sea salt

1 tsp baking powder

1 tbsp ground golden flax

1 tbsp hemp hearts

3 tbsp mini chocolate chips (optional)

Coconut oil (for frying; optional)

1. In a large bowl, mix the coconut oil and nut butter until smooth. Mix in honey or syrup if using.

2. Beat in the eggs one at a time until combined completely.

3. Whisk in the vanilla extract and apple cider vinegar and set aside.

4. In a separate bowl, mix the coconut flour, cinnamon, salt, baking powder, flax, hemp hearts, and chocolate chips, if using.

5. Place a nonstick or cast-iron pan on the stove and heat on medium-low (preheat it for a good few minutes). Melt the coconut oil into the pan if using. When the pan is hot, mix the wet ingredients with the dry and drop by the spoonful into the pan.

6. Cook each pancake until bubbles form and pop. Flip pancake over and cook until done, about 2 to 3 minutes total per cake. Serve immediately or cool and freeze on baking trays.

Waffles

There's nothing more comforting on lazy weekend mornings than the warm smell of waffles. These breakfast superstars contain zero refined sugar and are, of course, dairy- and grain-free, but you won't miss those aspects at all. Served straight out of the waffle iron with fresh berries and coconut cream, these light and fluffy beauties will have you wishing you were a kid again.

YIELD: 6–8 WAFFLES

¾ cup almond meal or flour

3 tbsp coconut flour

2 tbsp arrowroot flour

2 tbsp cocoa powder

1 tsp baking powder

¼ tsp sea salt

4 eggs

2 tbsp coconut oil, melted

⅓ cup coconut milk

1 tbsp honey

1 tbsp pure vanilla extract

3 tbsp or 1 oz 90 to 100 percent dark chocolate, chopped (optional)

2–3 tbsp coconut oil, melted (for greasing your waffle maker)

1. In a large bowl, blend the dry ingredients (all flours, cocoa, baking powder, and salt) until thoroughly combined.

2. In a separate, smaller bowl, combine the wet ingredients (excluding the chocolate) until thoroughly combined.

3. Scrape the wet ingredients into the dry and stir to combine. Stir in the chopped chocolate, if using, just before you are ready to cook.

4. Follow the directions for your waffle maker to preheat. Brush the melted coconut oil over the waffle iron on all sides. Spoon batter into each section and close the lid. Remove waffles when done (golden brown and cooked through).

5. Serve immediately or freeze on baking trays in a single layer and reheat in your toaster.

Black Forest Smoothie

Making smoothies is one of my favorite ways to make a quick meal on the go. When they have flavors like chocolate and cherries, it feels like you're somehow not being healthy, but you really are. This smoothie is packed with protein, antioxidants, healthy fats, and lots of carbs. It's perfect for first thing in the morning, or right before and right after a heavy workout. The key to not finding clumps of coconut oil in your smoothie is in the way you add it to the smoothie. See the instructions at right for the secret.

YIELD: 1 SERVING

½ cup almond or coconut milk

1 cup frozen sweet cherries, pitted

1 banana (preferably frozen)

4 large ice cubes

2 tsp cocoa powder

1 scoop (30 g) protein powder (any kind)

½ tsp pure vanilla extract

1 tbsp coconut oil, melted

1. Place all ingredients (except the coconut oil) in the blender in the order listed.

2. Set the blender to medium and allow mixture to get fairly smooth before adding the coconut oil.

3. Once it's smooth, open the pour spout at the top of most blenders (or remove the lid) and slowly pour in the liquid coconut oil as you blend.

4. Pour into a serving glass and drink up!

Apple-Maple-Bacon Granola

Granola used to be considered a healthy alternative to other cereals, but then we all found out how much sugar and other not-so-healthy stuff was actually in it. This granola, being grain-free, is quite calorie dense. Although it's low in sugar, it is quite high in protein and fat. Everyone in our household (and our neighbor's) can attest to the fact that it's much too easy to eat the whole batch in one evening. We try to eat it in small amounts during high-energy activities, like hiking, and the kids love it. Be warned, though, it's highly addictive!

YIELD: APPROXIMATELY 6 CUPS

8 slices thick-cut bacon, cooked but not crisp

2 cups coconut chips (ribbon coconut)

½ cup golden flax, ground

¼ cup hemp hearts or sesame seeds

1 cup raw sunflower seeds

⅓ cup each raw cashews, pecans, and hazelnuts,
    roughly chopped

⅓ cup coconut oil

3 tbsp maple syrup

1 tsp pure vanilla extract

½ tsp ground cinnamon

½ tsp sea salt

1 egg white

1 cup unsulfured apple rings (dried apple),
    roughly chopped

1. Preheat oven to 300°F. Line a large baking tray with parchment paper.

2. Chop or crumble the bacon into small chunks. In a large bowl, mix the bacon with the coconut chips, flax, hemp or sesame, sunflower seeds, and chopped nuts. Set aside.

3. In a small saucepan, melt the coconut oil with the maple syrup, vanilla, cinnamon, and sea salt. Pour this over the nut mixture and stir to combine.

4. Stir in the egg white, pour over the parchment-lined baking tray, and flatten out as best you can. It should be not too thick, or it won't crisp up. Bake for 25 minutes in the preheated oven.

5. Remove from the oven and cool for 20 minutes. Break into pieces, stir in the apple pieces, and store in an airtight container for up to 5 days.

Poached Eggs over Portobello Caps

Brunch is such a staple where I live. People line up for hours on Sunday mornings to get their spot at one of our city's finest brunch establishments. I prefer to stay at home, make some fresh coffee, crank up some tunes, and make my own from my neighbor's pastured eggs and whatever ingredients I have lying around. This dish, a Paleo-style eggs Benedict, seems complicated, but is worth every second of work. Plan a little in advance and you'll have a fabulous brunch to make for houseguests, on special occasions, or just as part of your regular Sunday routine.

YIELD: 4 SERVINGS

For the Not-Hollandaise Sauce

1 large avocado

Juice of 1 lemon

3 tbsp extra-virgin olive oil

2 tsp grainy Dijon mustard

Almond milk (for consistency)

For the Mushroom Filling

2 tbsp coconut oil

½ sweet onion, diced

3 oz fresh spinach, chopped

1 tbsp sundried tomatoes, minced

2 tsp coconut aminos

2 sprigs fresh thyme, leaves removed from stem and minced

For the Mushrooms Caps

4 portobello mushrooms

2 tbsp coconut oil, melted

1 clove garlic, minced or grated

2 sprigs thyme, minced

1 tbsp aged balsamic vinegar

For the Poached Eggs

4 cups water

1 tbsp white vinegar

4 pastured eggs

1. Make the Not-Hollandaise Sauce: In a food processor, place the avocado, lemon juice, olive oil, and Dijon. Blend until smooth, adding almond milk if desired for a runny sauce, and set aside until the last step.

2. Prepare the mushroom filling: In a sauté pan on medium heat, melt the coconut oil. Add in the onion and stir for 2 to 3 minutes or until the onions are softened. Add the spinach, sundried tomatoes, coconut aminos, and thyme and continue to sauté. Keep warm on stove while you prepare the remainder.

3. Prepare the mushroom caps: Preheat oven to 350°F. Remove the stems of the mushrooms and reserve. Remove the gills of the caps with a spoon by lightly scraping them away from the flesh.

4. Assemble the marinade for the mushrooms by mixing the coconut oil, garlic, thyme, and balsamic vinegar together. Brush over the caps, place on a baking sheet, and bake in the preheated oven for 10 minutes.

5. While the caps are baking, prepare the poached eggs: In a medium saucepan or pot, heat water on high heat until it boils. Add the vinegar and reduce to a simmer. While it's bubbling, crack an egg on a hard surface and then open the shell over the water (the shell should be almost touching the water). This

ensures that when the egg is cracked into the simmering water, it retains its rounded shape. All 4 eggs should be able to fit in the water at once, but make sure the water is simmering every time you add an egg. Each egg should take about 3 minutes for a soft poach, 5 for a medium poach, or 6 for hard yolks.

6. To assemble, remove the caps from the oven and place each one on a serving dish. Fill each cap with the stuffing mixture, then place a poached egg on top, followed by a spoonful of Not Hollandaise Sauce. Garnish with a sprig of thyme and serve.

Sweet Potato Cups with Baked Eggs

These little personal-size egg and potato dishes are perfect for portion control. You can make one or fourteen of them; just adjust the recipe as needed. They make a pretty impressive presentation and can be served along with some toasted sandwich bread for dipping and some crisped bacon for crunching. If you prefer a scrambled egg over a sunny-side-up one, whisk the eggs, oil, herbs, and salt and pepper before pouring over the sweet potatoes.

YIELD: 1 SERVING

4 to 5 oz grated sweet potato (about 1 small, 4-inch potato)

2 tbsp + 2 tsp coconut oil, melted and divided

1 tbsp fresh herbs (such as basil, rosemary, or chives), finely minced

1–2 pastured eggs

Sea salt and fresh-cracked pepper to taste

1. Preheat oven to 400°F.

2. Mix grated sweet potatoes with 2 tbsp of coconut oil. Pat into bottom and up sides of a 16-ounce baking dish or ramekin.

3. Bake sweet potato for 25 to 30 minutes or until golden and crisp on the edges.

4. Remove from oven and sprinkle in herbs. Crack eggs directly over herbs and pour remaining oil over. Season with salt and pepper and place back in oven for 6 to 8 minutes or until eggs are cooked to your desired doneness.

Caveman Porridge

The consistency of this "porridge" is truly like a big bowl of a certain childhood favorite of mine, which my parents would fill full of plump, juicy raisins and serve with a cold shot of milk. It has a sort of stick-to-your-ribs goodness served by itself, but topped with nut butter, honey, nuts, coconut butter, fresh fruit, or even yogurt, this recipe really shines. You could even add in some cocoa or frozen berries during the cooking process for a real treat. So go ahead, experiment—you'll be eating like a caveman in no time.

YIELD: 1 SERVING

1 tbsp coconut oil

1 medium banana, mashed

¾ cup egg whites (or the whites from 12 eggs)

½ cup almond or coconut milk

2 tbsp golden flax, ground

2 tsp hemp hearts

1 tsp pure vanilla extract

½ tsp ground cinnamon

Pinch sea salt

1–2 tbsp coconut or almond butter (optional)

1. In a small saucepan, melt the coconut oil over low heat. Add the mashed banana to the coconut oil. Raise the heat to medium. Cook, stirring continuously, for 3 to 4 minutes or until banana begins to smell caramelized and has a golden color to it.

2. In a separate bowl, mix the egg whites, milk, flax, and hemp. Pour the mixture into the small saucepan with the banana and mix thoroughly. Use a stick blender for a better consistency, or a whisk, but watch for lumps.

3. Add the remaining ingredients (except for the coconut or almond butter) and blend until smooth.

4. Over medium-high heat, whisk the porridge continuously for 5 to 8 minutes. The porridge should become creamy and somewhat lumpy. Keep whisking until it is too thick to whisk anymore.

5. Pour into a serving bowl, top with coconut or almond butter, if using, and serve immediately. (You can also refrigerate for up to 24 hours for a tasty cold treat topped with fruit.)

Salads and Dressings

Apple and Fennel Slaw

In the culinary world, there are many beautiful pairs: salt and pepper, orange and vanilla, fish and lemon. Then there is this one: apple and fennel. The crisp sweet/tart of the apple and the mellow yet vibrant licorice of the fennel, when paired with the creamy dressing, make for an explosion of fresh and summery flavors that has become quite a favorite in our house.

YIELD: 6–8 SERVINGS

For the Dressing

½ cup coconut oil mayonnaise (see page 27)

Juice of one lemon

1 tsp Dijon mustard

1 tbsp apple cider vinegar

1 tsp honey

1 tsp poppy seeds

¼ tsp sea salt

Fresh-cracked pepper

½ tsp onion powder

For the Salad

1 fennel bulb

2 tart apples

1. For the dressing: Whisk the mayonnaise with the lemon and Dijon. Add remaining ingredients and whisk until smooth. Set aside until needed.

2. For the salad: Cut the top and bottom off the fennel. Cut in half, then into quarters. Slice into very thin shreds and place in a large bowl.

3. Peel and core the apples and cut into very thin slices or matchsticks. Combine with fennel, pour dressing over, toss to combine, and serve.

Avocado-Pesto Dressing

Without the aid of dairy products, it is often hard to achieve a "creamy" consistency in recipes such as dressings, ice cream, dips, and sauces. One of the many ways in which to achieve a creamy consistency when avoiding dairy or soy products is to use avocado. Raw avocado, when blended and mixed with strong flavors, lends an incredibly rich and creamy mouth feel to many dishes. I love to use avocado in dressings and sauces and even desserts too! This dressing is amazing on salads, as a dip, and over chicken or fish, just to name a few uses.

YIELD: APPROXIMATELY 1½ CUPS

1 large ripe avocado (about ¾ cup),
   pitted and peeled

½ cup loosely packed fresh basil

½ cup loosely packed fresh cilantro

1 clove garlic

Juice of 1 lemon

Juice of 1 lime

½ cup olive oil

½ cup coconut oil, melted

1 tbsp red wine vinegar

2 tbsp apple cider vinegar

½ tsp sea salt

1. In a blender or food processor add the avocado, herbs, garlic, and citrus. Pulse until mostly smooth.

2. Set the blender to medium low and slowly pour in the oils in a drizzle, one at a time. The process to completely add the oils should take about 10 minutes.

3. Finish by adding the vinegars and salt.

4. This dressing is best used immediately but can be stored for a day in the refrigerator.

Roasted Butternut Squash Salad with Lime and Cilantro Dressing

Squash is not often used in salads, but it has a beautifully complex flavor that pairs well with lime and the sweet notes of honey. Make this salad right before you are planning on serving it as the squash can get mushy when it sits too long. If you plan on storing it for more than an hour, keep the vegetables and dressing separated at room temperature. Combine just before serving.

YIELD: 4 SERVINGS

For the Salad

2 medium butternut squash

1 medium sweet onion

2 tbsp coconut oil

Sea salt and fresh-cracked black pepper to taste

For the Dressing

Juice of 1 lime (or 3–4 Key limes)

Zest of ½ lime (or 2 Key limes)

2 tbsp raw honey

Small handful fresh cilantro, minced

1. Preheat oven to 400°F. Peel and dice the squash and onion into approximately 1-inch cubes.

2. Melt the coconut oil and toss with the onion and squash. Season with salt and pepper, toss again, and pour out onto a large baking tray in one even layer.

3. Roast for 30 to 35 minutes, tossing halfway through, until vegetables are softened and slightly golden.

4. Remove from oven and cool on tray to room temperature.

5. Make the dressing: Mix dressing ingredients (except cilantro) together in a small saucepan over low heat. Heat until honey dissolves into lime juice. Remove from heat and stir in cilantro.

6. Pour over salad and serve warm.

Caesar Salad

My family has had a long love affair with Caesar salad. Every year, on our respective birthdays, we were given the choice of whatever gastronomical delight we could imagine. Usually this involved one of my mother's delectable specialties, which included the most decadent lasagna, steamed crab with garlic butter, artichokes, or Caesar salad with loads of dressing. I always picked Caesar salad and lasagna, usually with a big helping of garlic bread. Now that I live a gluten-free life, croutons are not a part of my Caesar. If you feel like your salad needs more crunch, cook some bacon to a crispy finish and crumble over your salad. This dressing is not ideal for make-ahead occasions, as refrigerating it will cause the coconut oil to solidify. It's best for making and serving immediately.

YIELD: 4–6 SERVINGS

2 egg yolks, coddled*
2 tbsp Dijon mustard
¼ cup + 2 tbsp coconut oil, melted
2 tbsp red wine vinegar
2 tbsp capers, minced
1 clove garlic, minced or grated
Sea salt and fresh-cracked pepper to taste
1 tbsp anchovy paste in olive oil or 3–4 fillets
in olive oil, minced

1 tsp coconut aminos
Juice of ½ lemon
1–2 heads Romaine lettuce, cut or ripped
into pieces
2 tsp nutritional yeast or grated Parmesan
(optional)

To coddle an egg yolk: Have your eggs at room temperature (otherwise, when you pour the boiling water over them, they will crack). Boil some water and pour over the whole eggs. Allow them to sit in the hot water for 10 minutes. The egg will still be raw, but the yolks will have a slightly thicker, creamier consistency.

1. In a large bowl, combine the coddled egg yolks and Dijon. Whisk together until smooth.

2. Slowly, very slowly, whisk in the liquid coconut oil a little at a time, until all is combined.

3. Whisk in remaining ingredients (except lettuce and yeast or Parmesan) and serve immediately over cold Romaine lettuce. Garnish with yeast or Parmesan.

Coconut Oil Mayonnaise

This mayonnaise is amazing. The flavors of the coconut oil and the olive oil combine to create a very creamy, rich, and wonderfully versatile base for dressings or sauces, and even for use on sandwiches! Store in an airtight container for three to seven days.

YIELD: 1½ CUPS

2 egg yolks from pastured hens

2 tsp Dijon mustard

Juice of 1 lemon

½ tsp sea salt

½ cup coconut oil, melted

½ cup extra-virgin olive oil

1. In the jar of a blender or bowl of a food processor, combine the yolks, Dijon mustard, lemon juice, and sea salt until smooth.

2. With the motor running at medium speed, begin to pour the melted coconut oil into the blender or processor in a very fine stream. You will almost be dripping the oil in. It should take a good 5 minutes to emulsify all the coconut oil. When you've finished with the coconut oil, continue the same process with the olive oil. Don't be tempted to pour the oil faster, or risk breaking your mayonnaise.

3. Once all the oil has been combined with the other ingredients, pour into a jar and store in the refrigerator.

Fennel and Citrus Salad

Being that fennel makes an appearance a few times in this book, you may have guessed it's one of my favorite vegetables. In the summertime, this stuff grows on the side of the road where I live. It's abundant, refreshing, and adds texture and vibrant flavors to many dishes. A favorite of mine is to eat it raw in salads. Paired with other refreshing flavors, like apple or citrus, the fennel really shines. This salad is a perfect accompaniment to fish dishes or even as a topper for a leafy salad.

YIELD: 4 SERVINGS

For the Salad

2 large fennel bulbs

4 navel oranges, segmented or supremed*

For the Dressing

¼ cup coconut oil mayonnaise

1 tbsp Dijon mustard

1 tbsp honey

¼ cup extra-virgin olive oil

1 tsp poppy seeds

Juice and zest of 1 lemon

¼ tsp sea salt

Fresh-cracked pepper to taste

1 tbsp apple cider vinegar

*To Supreme an Orange: First slice off the top and bottom of the orange (just enough to break through the membrane). Then, sliding your knife just under the skin, cut off all the skin and membrane from the outside of the orange, following the shape of the fruit. Now, find each membrane (the piece of skin that separates each segment), slide your knife in next to it, and cut. Now do the same on the other side of the same segment. This should free the segment of orange from the membrane. Voilà, a supreme! Now continue to do this for all the oranges.

1. Prepare the salad: Slice the fennel tops and fronds away from the bulb and either compost them, use them as garnish, or save the stalks for use in soups (like celery). Cut the bulb in half, lay the cut side down on a cutting board, and slice as thinly as possible. Toss into a bowl and set aside.

2. Toss the oranges in with the fennel and set aside while you make the dressing.

3. Make the dressing: Mix the mayonnaise, Dijon, and honey together until combined. Slowly whisk in the olive oil until smooth. Mix in the remaining ingredients, toss with the orange and fennel, and serve immediately.

Jicama and Mango Salad

The jicama, also known as a Mexican turnip, is a crunchy and refreshing tuber native to Mexico, where it is often served with lime and chili powder. The flavor can be described as similar to that of a water chestnut, except with slightly more sweetness and a little more of a refreshing burst of liquid when you bite into it. It is a great addition to any salad or can simply be eaten as a snack. The addition of an acid (such as citrus juice) can prevent browning due to oxidizing after cutting, much like apples or potatoes. The dressing for this salad is versatile and can be dramatically changed by simply adding in different fresh herbs. Here, cilantro gives a Mexican feel while the basil gives it a much sweeter flavor.

YIELD: 4–6 SIDE SERVINGS

For the Salad

1 large jicama (1½–2 pounds)

2 ataulfo mangoes

For the Dressing

1 tbsp + 1 tsp Dijon mustard

¼ cup coconut oil, melted

Juice of 1 lime (approximately 3 tbsp)

2 tbsp honey

2 tbsp fresh cilantro or basil, minced

Sea salt and fresh-cracked pepper to taste

2 tbsp apple cider vinegar

1 tbsp red wine vinegar

1. Peel the jicama with a small paring knife by removing the top and bottom first and then removing the remaining peel. Cut the jicama into bite-size cubes and set aside in a bowl.

2. Cube the mango (see note). Add to jicama and set aside.

3. Make the dressing: In a food processor or blender, place the Dijon. Set the speed to medium and slowly pour in the coconut oil in a fine stream or drips. If you go too quickly, the dressing will separate.

4. Once you have added all the coconut oil, add the remaining ingredients and blend until combined.

5. Toss the dressing with the jicama and mango and serve immediately.

Note: To cube a mango, set it on its thinnest edge. You want the pit to run parallel to the knife when you cut in. Estimate the size of the pit and try to slip the knife in next to it. (You can also push the tip of the knife in to find the pit.) Slice off the sides of the mango next to the pit. Holding the cut mango segment in the palm of your hand, lightly push the knife into the flesh (being careful not to go too deep). Run a crisscross pattern into the mango, creating little cubes. Now push the skin up from the other side, essentially turning the mango inside out. Now cut off the cubes with the knife and set them in the bowl with the jicama. Continue the same process with the other halves.

Zucchini Noodle Salad

Pasta salad during the summer is as quintessential as pumpkin pie at Thanksgiving: It's just not the same without it. Living grain- and gluten-free can make having this dish quite a task. There are some options out there, mainly seaweed or yam noodles, but using zucchini noodles is quite a bit more economical, and during the bountiful summer months, anything that uses up zucchini from the garden is a friend. This salad is much easier to make using a spiral slicer, available at specialty kitchen stores or online, but if you can't find one, just use a mandoline or even a box grater.

YIELD: 6–8 SERVINGS

For the Salad

1 pound zucchini

3–4 white or brown mushrooms, sliced

1–2 mini cucumbers (or half a large, long English), sliced

¾ cup cherry or grape tomatoes, halved

1 large avocado, cut into small chunks

¼ cup fresh herbs (basil, chives, cilantro, etc.), minced

4 radishes, sliced

For the Dressing

¼ cup coconut oil mayonnaise

1 tbsp coconut or apple cider vinegar

Sea salt and fresh-cracked pepper to taste

1 tbsp (or more) almond milk

1 tsp Dijon mustard

1. Make the salad: Slice the zucchini with a spiral slicer, grater, or mandoline into long, thin strips. If using a grater, squeeze out excess liquid. Place in a large bowl with remaining salad ingredients.

2. Make the dressing: Mix the mayonnaise with the vinegar, salt, pepper, almond milk, and Dijon. Whisk to combine and toss with the salad. Serve immediately. (If storing, keep salad and dressing separate until just before serving.)

Roasted Broccoli, Bacon, and Sunflower Salad

Broccoli is not everyone's favorite vegetable, but add a couple of ingredients and suddenly this cruciferous vegetable is transformed into a picky-eater pleaser! Bacon just makes everything better and in this salad it truly shines as a star. Matched with the sweet notes of balsamic, the sharp flavor of the garlic and Dijon, and the crunch of sunflower seeds, bacon and broccoli marry together into a perfect accompaniment to most any main dish. This is a favorite in our house for those quick-to-throw-together dinner-party dishes.

YIELD: 4–6 SERVINGS

1 pound broccoli (about 1 large broccoli), cut into florets

6 slices thick-cut bacon, diced

2 tbsp raw, hulled sunflower seeds

½ sweet onion, diced

1 clove garlic, minced or grated

1 tsp Dijon mustard

2 tbsp coconut oil, melted

2 tbsp aged balsamic vinegar

Sea salt and fresh-cracked pepper to taste

1. Preheat oven to 400°F. Mix broccoli with bacon, sunflower seeds, onion, and garlic in a baking dish and cover with a lid or aluminum foil.

2. In a separate bowl, mix the Dijon, coconut oil, balsamic vinegar, and salt and pepper to form a dressing. Pour over the bacon-broccoli mixture and place in the oven.

3. Bake, covered, for 20 minutes, stirring occasionally. Remove cover and bake another 15 minutes or until bacon is cooked through and broccoli is golden on the edges. Serve.

Salt-Roasted Beet Salad with Honey-Lemon-Vanilla Dressing

Beets are a pain for most people. They stain your hands, your clothes, and your cutting boards, you have to peel them, and what do you do with the tops? This recipe solves a lot of the worst parts of this amazing root. You can either buy bulk beets (that's what they call them when they are just the root, no tops), or buy them with tops on; simply remove the greens and cook them as you would kale or spinach. In this recipe, roasting the beets inside an enclosed dish atop a bed of salt permeates the beets with flavor. When they are done, you simply slip off the skins and slice them up. This is a great salad for impressing guests. The colors and flavors make a great match for a summer gathering.

YIELD: 4–6 SERVINGS

For the Beets

2 pounds beets (any kind), skin on and tops removed

Kosher, rock, or coarse sea salt

6 sprigs fresh thyme

For the Dressing

½ cup coconut oil mayonnaise

Juice of 2 lemons

Zest of 1 lemon

1 clove garlic, minced or grated

2 tbsp honey

1 tsp pure vanilla extract

For the Salad

5–8 oz mixed greens (spinach, arugula, mixed lettuces, etc.)

1 cup walnut or other nut pieces, chopped

1–2 large avocados, diced

1. Prepare the beets: Preheat oven to 400°F. Fill a shallow 9 x 13-inch baking dish with just enough salt to cover the bottom. Lay the beets over the salt, followed by the thyme. Cover with aluminum foil or a lid and roast in the oven for 1 hour. Beets are done when the tip of a sharp knife inserted into the middle meets little to no resistance.

2. Remove from heat, uncover, and allow to cool to room temperature. Slip the skins off and slice into wedges. Set aside until needed.

3. Make the dressing: Whisk all the ingredients together and let stand while you assemble the salad.

4. Compose the salad: For the most aesthetic results, lay the salad greens on individual plates, topped with the nuts and the avocado. Scatter the beets over and dress with the dressing.

5. Serve.

Sides

Caramelized Carrots

Carrots are often overlooked for side dishes, being relegated to stick form in kids' lunches and crudités platters. Here they shine in a very simple dish, allowing their sweetness to be amplified by a slight touch of maple syrup. The more you stir, the less the carrots will get that beautiful golden touch. So resist the temptation to stir too often and just allow the carrots to sit for a few minutes at a time as they cook.

YIELD: 4 SERVINGS

1½–2 pounds carrots, peeled and cut into bite-size
    chunks (any style will do)
1 tsp maple syrup
2 tbsp coconut oil
Sea salt to taste

1. Toss the carrots in a bowl with the maple syrup.

2. In a large, heavy-bottomed frying pan (preferably cast iron), heat coconut oil over medium-high heat.

3. Pour the carrots into the pan and sauté for 20 to 25 minutes, stirring occasionally. You may need to reduce the heat to medium, depending on your stove and the frying pan you are using. The carrots need to cook at a fairly high temperature to achieve caramelization, but they need ample time to cook through as well.

4. Season with sea salt to taste and serve.

Cinnamon Fried Plantains

Plantains, though quite popular in African, South American, and Caribbean cuisines, are not that well known in most parts of North America. This versatile fruit, of the same family as the banana, can be eaten at any stage of ripeness. When green, the plantain is similar in flavor and consistency to a potato and can be used in any way a starchy potato would be. When a deep yellow color is achieved and black spots begin to appear, the plantain really comes alive for sweet dishes. For this dish, choose plantains that are dark yellow to almost black for optimal sweetness.

YIELD: 4–6 SERVINGS

2 large plantains

2 tbsp coconut oil

½ tsp ground cinnamon

Sea salt to taste

1. To peel a ripe plantain, slice through the skin with a knife, vertically, from stem to tip. Open the peel like a suit jacket and peel away. Slice the plantains into thick chips or chunks.

2. In a heavy-bottomed frying pan, heat the coconut oil on medium heat. Place the plantains in the hot oil and sprinkle with cinnamon and sea salt. Turn every 3 to 4 minutes to make sure nothing is burning, and continue to cook until all sides are golden brown and caramelized (about 15 minutes).

3. Serve immediately.

Curried Cauliflower Steaks

Curry dishes are a favorite in our house, especially in cooler winter months. There's just something comforting about the rich, warm smell of a cooking curry. We cook up these thick cauliflower steaks and serve them with roasted chicken, pork chops, or lamb. If you like the feel of a creamy curry, add ½ cup coconut milk in the last step, about 4 minutes before the end of cooking. You will have a rich, decadent curry that can be eaten alone or with a good chunk of protein.

YIELD: 4 SERVINGS

2 tbsp coconut oil

2 tsp garlic, minced or grated

2 tsp fresh ginger, minced or grated

1 tsp cumin seeds

½ tsp ground coriander

½ tsp sea salt

Pinch of cayenne (or more if you like it hot!)

2 tsp ground turmeric

14-oz can diced tomatoes (no salt added)

¾ cup water

1 head cauliflower, cut into thick steaks
   (see note)

Note: Have everything prepped and ready to go before starting. This recipe moves quickly once you get started and you'll need everything at hand to make it easy for yourself. To cut cauliflower into steaks: Cut away all leaves and set cauliflower stem-end down. Slice the cauliflower like a loaf of bread, making steaks about ¾ inch thick. The slices closer to the ends will most likely fall apart, but don't worry about that.

1. Heat oil over medium-high heat in a large, deep saucepan or pot with a tight-fitting lid.

2. When oil is hot, add the garlic and ginger and stir until golden brown.

3. Add dried spices, turn down to medium heat, and cook, stirring constantly, for 5 to 6 minutes.

4. Turn heat down to medium low, add tomatoes and water, and cook for 5 to 8 minutes. You'll know it's ready when the tomatoes and spices start to meld and give off an incredible scent.

5. Add cauliflower steaks, cover with lid, and cook 10 to 15 minutes.

6. Remove lid, transfer to serving dish, and serve immediately.

Hasselback Sweet Potatoes

Although these are really just fancy baked sweet potatoes, the extra steps taken to create the Hasselback effect makes them extra fun for parties and get-togethers. They also have more surface area to become crispy on the edges yet buttery on the inside. The key to not cutting all the way through the potato is to lay two chopsticks down next to your potato (you can even cut off a bit of the bottom of the potato to keep it sturdy) and when you slice down, you won't be able to go all the way.

YIELD: 6 SERVINGS

2 pounds small sweet potatoes (orange fleshed)

3 tbsp coconut oil, melted

Sea salt to taste

1 tsp ground cinnamon (optional)

1. Preheat the oven to 400°F. Cut the ends off each potato (and a small bit at the bottom if you want them to stay put better). Slice the potato into segments crosswise, not cutting all the way through, so you have a fan-like effect (see headnote for my chopstick trick for this).

2. Pour or brush the melted coconut oil over the potatoes (trying to get in all the nooks and crannies). Sprinkle the salt and optional cinnamon (if using) over them and place on a baking sheet. Bake for 35 to 45 minutes or until slightly golden on the edges and soft throughout.

3. Serve immediately.

Sweet Potato–Coconut Casserole

Sweet potatoes in casserole form are often served at Thanksgiving gatherings as "candied," with brown sugar and marshmallow topping, or with pecans and brown sugar, but for me the sweet potato is sweet enough by itself! In this iteration of a sweet potato casserole, the nuts have been replaced with crispy coconut chips and there is no sugar in sight (although there is a hint of honey). Serve alongside your usual Thanksgiving dishes or as a comforting side dish anytime.

YIELD: 8 SERVINGS

7–8 medium sweet potatoes (2 pounds)

2 tbsp coconut oil, melted

2 eggs

¼ tsp sea salt

½ tsp ground cinnamon

¼ tsp ground nutmeg

¼ tsp ground cardamom

¼ tsp ground ginger

1 tbsp honey

1 tsp pure vanilla extract

½ cup coconut chips, flakes, or ribbons, for topping

1. Preheat oven to 400°F. Peel and cube sweet potatoes.

2. Mix the peeled sweet potatoes with the melted coconut oil and pour into a shallow roasting dish. Cover and roast for 30 to 40 minutes, or until soft.

3. Remove from oven and mash with a potato masher or immersion blender. Leave the oven on. Allow the mashed potatoes to cool slightly (5 minutes) at room temperature.

4. Mix the remaining ingredients, except the coconut chips, into the mash and blend well. Pour into a shallow roasting dish and place back into the oven for 15 to 20 minutes.

5. Take the potatoes out a few minutes before serving, sprinkle the coconut-chip topping over, and return to oven. Remove when topping is slightly golden. Serve immediately.

Italian Cauliflower "Couscous"

Since we don't consume grains in our house, side dishes can get a little, er, routine now and then. We love our plantains and sweet potatoes, but sometimes you really just crave a familiar dish that you had years ago, or at least something similar. To me that was a warm bowl of Italian couscous served with fresh basil. True couscous is not a grain but is made from grains, and is actually little itty-bitty balls of pasta that are traditionally hand-rolled. The dish I created to remind me of that fragrant comfort food is often called cauliflower rice in gluten-free circles. I find the texture is a lot more like couscous than rice, so that is what we call it. This dish is easy to make and makes great leftovers for fried "rice" the next day!

YIELD: 6–8 SERVINGS

1 large head cauliflower, cut into 3–4 pieces
     and trimmed of green leaves
2 tbsp coconut oil
1 clove garlic, minced or grated
1 small sweet onion, diced
4 mushrooms, diced
1 sweet red pepper, seeded and diced
Small handful fresh basil leaves, minced or
     torn into small pieces
Sea salt and fresh-cracked pepper to taste

1. In a blender or food processor, pulse the cauliflower pieces until they resemble rice. Set aside in a bowl.

2. In a large frying pan or Dutch oven (big enough to contain all the cauliflower), heat the coconut oil on medium heat. Add the garlic, onion, mushrooms, and pepper. Sauté for 5 to 7 minutes or until all are softened and slightly golden.

3. Add the cauliflower and continue to sauté for at least another 10 minutes or until the cauliflower has softened completely. Toss in the basil and season with salt and pepper to taste.

4. Serve immediately.

Mashed Fauxtatoes

We're not huge fans of regular white potatoes around here, most often replacing them with sweet potatoes for roasting, baking, chip making, and the like. But when it comes to mashed potatoes, the orange-fleshed tubers just aren't the same. Over the years, I've experimented with numerous combinations of white vegetables to try to get that fluffy consistency. The underutilized celery root (the underground portion of our friend celery), though, makes for an almost identical fluffy bowl of steaming hot mash. Serve with roasted meats and their juices for a real treat.

YIELD: 4–6 SERVINGS

1 pound celery root (celeriac), peeled and cubed

2 tbsp coconut oil

1 tsp truffle oil (optional but tasty!)

Sea salt and fresh-cracked pepper to taste

1. Fill a large pot, fitted with a steamer basket, with 3 inches of water. Bring to a boil and fill the basket with the celery root. Steam for 10 to 15 minutes.

2. Remove from the steamer, and mash with an immersion blender or in a blender (manual mashers will not create the right consistency). Pulse the celery root so that you do not overmix it.

3. Stir in the coconut oil and truffle oil (if using) and season with salt and pepper.

4. Serve immediately.

Roasted Garlic Fennel

Fennel is a vegetable that not many people have had or know what to do with. It's one of my favorite summer veggies because it is quite versatile. Raw, roasted, steamed, mashed, pureed, or grilled, this vegetable can do it all. Native to the Mediterranean, but cultivated in many areas, Florence fennel (the variety that produces a bulb) is quite popular in modern cuisine. Here, it is left to shine as the star of the dish. Roasting mellows the flavor of both the fennel and the garlic and leaves a nice, faint anise flavor when finished. This dish is perfect for pairing with chicken, fish, or pork.

YIELD: 4–6 SERVINGS

2 large fennel bulbs

5 large cloves of garlic, peeled

Sea salt and fresh-cracked pepper to taste

2 tbsp coconut oil, melted

1. Preheat oven to 400°F. Slice fennel greens (tops) off bulbs, if needed. You can chop them up for salads or use as a garnish for this dish. Cut bulbs into wedges.

2. Place fennel, garlic, salt, pepper, and coconut oil into a roasting dish and cover with a tight-fitting lid or aluminum foil.

3. Bake for 35 to 45 minutes total, removing lid or foil after 25 minutes.

4. Serve immediately.

Zucchini Pancakes

Zucchini is a wonderful vegetable (botanically speaking, though, it's actually a fruit!). Not only is it packed with folate, potassium, manganese, and vitamin A, but it is useful in savory and sweet recipes. One of my favorite foods as a kid was a chocolate zucchini loaf made by my aunt. I have found, though, that most people prefer their zucchini in savory dishes and cooked. I could eat it raw any day of the week, but some people find it bitter or not overly pleasant. Making it into pancakes, however, seems to appeal to even the pickiest of consumers. In the peak of summer, when zucchini takes over your garden, making these as often as possible is a good way to keep up with their overabundance.

YIELD: 10–12 PANCAKES

1 pound zucchini (about 3 medium zucchinis)

3 eggs

Sea salt and fresh-cracked pepper to taste

2 tbsp–¼ cup coconut oil

1 clove garlic, minced or grated

Zest of ½ lemon

1 tsp baking powder

2 tbsp chopped chives or spring onions

2 tbsp coconut flour

1. Grate the zucchini on the largest side of a box grater or in a food processor. Squeeze out the excess moisture and place in a bowl.

2. In a small bowl, whisk the eggs and season with salt and pepper. Stir into the grated zucchini.

3. In a nonstick pan, melt the coconut oil over medium-high heat. (If you don't think you will be able to put the whole batch of pancakes in the pan at one time, preheat your oven to 300°F and put a baking pan on one of the racks to hold the first batch while you cook the remainder.)

4. Add the remaining ingredients to the zucchini-egg mixture.

5. Scoop out some of the batter and place in the hot oil. Continue until the pan is full, with enough room to flip the pancakes. Cook each pancake for 2 to 3 minutes per side. Transfer to oven for holding or onto plates for serving. Serve immediately.

Mains

Cauliflower-Crusted Pizza

When I used to eat grains, I was pretty hardcore about my breadstuffs. I made my own bread (I had my own sourdough starter in the fridge), my own pizza crusts, my own English muffins! I miss those old-time favorites, and while this does not replace my craving completely—the crust is not super sturdy and you'll most likely be eating it with a fork and a knife—the flavor is there. In fact, it is pretty astonishing how much it tastes like real pizza and that it's made from vegetables. Even my kids love it!

YIELD: 1 BIG PIZZA PIE (4–6 SERVINGS)

For the Crust

1 large head cauliflower, cut into chunks (not uniform)

2 eggs

1 tsp nutritional yeast

1 tsp dried oregano

2 tbsp coconut oil, melted

½ tsp sea salt

For Pizza Topping

Tomato or pizza sauce

6–8 mushrooms, sliced and sautéed

1 onion, sliced into half moons and caramelized

Chorizo sausage or other cured meat, sliced

Asparagus or sweet peppers, cut into chunks

2–3 cups grated cheese

1. Preheat the oven to 425°F. Wrap aluminum foil around a pizza stone or over a large, round pizza-baking sheet and rub a bit of coconut oil all over it. Set aside.

2. Set a pot fitted with a steamer insert and filled one third of the way with water on high heat. In a blender or food processor, pulse the cauliflower chunks until they resemble snow. When the water is boiling, put the cauliflower snow in the steamer and steam for 5 minutes.

3. Remove the cauliflower and pour into a mesh strainer. Squeeze the cauliflower against the sides of the mesh, straining out all the excess liquid. (The more liquid you can get out of it, the crispier your crust will be.)

4. Mix the cauliflower with the eggs, yeast, oregano, coconut oil, and salt. Pat it out onto the greased sheet of aluminum in a circular shape. Bake in the preheated oven for 35 to 45 minutes or until the crust is golden on the edges and completely cooked right through the center. Remove from the oven and add your toppings.

5. Spread the sauce you are using onto the crust. Evenly distribute all the toppings you are using (except cheese) over the sauce. Sprinkle cheese over the whole thing and return to the 425°F oven for 10 to 15 minutes. Remove from oven and allow to cool for 5 minutes. Slice with a pizza cutter and serve.

Fish "Tacos" with Coconut Flour Sopes and Pico de Gallo

Fish tacos have a long history along the western coast of Mexico, most abundantly on the Baja Peninsula. Travelers willing to venture to the quiet side of the popular tourist destination have long known that the best fish tacos come from small stands along the beaches in Ensenada and San Felipe. Here you'll find fresh-caught fish lightly deep-fried and served in either corn or flour tortillas with shredded cabbage, a thin mayonnaise-based sauce, a bit of salsa, and a squeeze of lime. My parents, retired and living in their RV part-time in Baja, brought this recipe home to me a few years back. In my version, the fish is grilled, the taco shells are really thick, grain-free sopes, and they are just as delicious.

YIELD: 6 SERVINGS

For the Pico de Gallo

½ sweet onion, diced very finely

1 Roma tomato, seeded and diced very finely

Juice of ½ lime

Sriracha to taste or ½ fresh jalapeño, seeded and diced very finely

2 tbsp fresh cilantro, minced

For the Sopes

¾ cup arrowroot flour

¾ cup coconut flour

1 tsp sea salt

¼ cup coconut oil

½ cup lard or palm shortening

½ cup cold water

1 egg + 3 tbsp egg whites

For the Filling

1 tbsp coconut oil, melted

½ tsp ground cumin

½ tsp ground coriander

1 tsp sea salt

1 tsp chili powder

2–3 fillets (approximately 1½ pounds) white fish (snapper, halibut, etc.)

2 Key limes, cut in half

For Serving

Shredded lettuce

Shredded cheese

Sour cream or plain yogurt

Mayonnaise

1. Make the pico de gallo: Mix all ingredients together and set aside in a non-reactive bowl.

2. Prepare the sopes: Mix flours and salt in a small bowl. With a pastry cutter, cut in the oil and lard or shortening.

3. In a separate bowl, mix water with eggs.

4. Blend water/egg mixture with flour mixture and work together with hands until combined.

5. Roll out into balls slightly larger than golf balls and flatten in palm of hand until about ½ inch thick at edges.

6. In a hot, dry pan (nonstick or cast iron) fry the sopes until golden, flipping only once.

7. Hold in a warm oven or a tortilla warmer until needed.

8. Prepare the filling: Preheat oven to 375°F. Brush oil onto large 9 x 13-inch baking tray.

9. In a small bowl blend spices together to combine.

10. Lay fish in baking pan and sprinkle with spice blend. Squeeze limes over and bake in preheated oven for 10 to 15 minutes or until fish is firm but not dry.

11. Serve fish on the sopes, with pico de gallo and lettuce, cheese, sour cream or plain yogurt, and mayonnaise

Crispy Almond Chicken Thighs

Deep-frying chicken (or anything for that matter) can seem like a daunting task, but by using a smaller pot and less oil, you end up wasting less food and not having a huge vat of oil to deal with in the end. By only deep-frying for the first few minutes, the chicken has a chance to crisp up in drier conditions in the oven, thus allowing the fat to drip away. This makes for an exceptionally crunchy coating and a very tender bite to the meat inside. Add any seasonings you want into the coating before you begin for a customized flavor.

YIELD: 4–6 SERVINGS

1 cup coconut oil

1¼ cups almond meal

3 tbsp arrowroot flour

½ tsp sea salt

Fresh-cracked pepper to taste

¼ cup almond milk

1 egg

8 chicken thighs (bone in and skin on)

1. In a small saucepan, on medium-high heat, melt the coconut oil. Preheat the oven to 400°F. Prepare a baking pan with a wire rack sitting on top of it. Place this in the preheated oven.

2. On a plate or in a shallow bowl, mix the almond meal, arrowroot, salt, and pepper.

3. In a small bowl, whisk the almond milk and egg to form an egg wash.

4. Dip the thighs into the egg wash, let the excess drip off a bit, and then dip into the almond meal mixture (2 at a time works best). Drop into the hot oil for 1 minute per side. Transfer each thigh to the baking sheet and repeat until all the thighs are in the oven.

5. Bake the thighs for 35 minutes in the preheated oven (the internal temperature should reach 160 to 165°F). Remove from oven and serve immediately.

Perfect Roasted Chicken

Perfectly moist, succulent chicken is possible without undercooking and certainly without overcooking. The trick to perfect roasted chicken is to rub the outside with oil for a crispy skin and place herbs, garlic, and lemon in the cavity. The lemon acts like a little steam maker, permeating the meat with a hint of citrus, while the herbs and garlic flavor everything just the way you like it. Roasting the bird with its breast down allows all the fat from the back to drip down the body, basting it as it roasts and ensuring it doesn't dry out.

YIELD: 4–6 SERVINGS

1 roasting chicken (3–5 pounds)

½ lemon

¼ cup fresh herbs (rosemary, thyme, oregano, sage, etc.)

4–5 cloves garlic, peeled and slightly crushed

2 tbsp coconut oil

Fine sea salt (Himalayan, Celtic, fleur de sel, etc.) and fresh-cracked black pepper to taste

1. Preheat your oven to 425°F. Dry the outside of the chicken with paper towels (or a designated cloth towel).

2. Place the lemon, herbs, and garlic into the cavity of the chicken.

3. Rub the outside of the chicken with the coconut oil and season with salt and pepper on all sides.

4. Set the chicken breast side down in a Dutch oven.

5. Roast uncovered in the preheated oven until a thermometer stuck in the thickest part of the thigh reads 165°F. Do not overcook (check at 30-minute intervals. Once you've made this recipe a few times, it becomes a lot easier to guess how long a chicken will take).

6. Let rest 20 minutes before carving.

Sweet Potato–Crusted Quiche

Quiche is a perfect egg dish for anyone afraid to cook eggs. Though things can go wrong in most any recipe (even boiling water!), quiche is pretty forgiving in its simplicity. Crack some eggs, whisk them up with various ingredients, pour onto a crust, and bake until the center is slightly jiggly. My only problem with quiche was always the grain-based crust. So in this recipe I improvised with sweet potato, which creates an equally delicious breakfast (or dinner!) staple.

YIELD: 6–8 SERVINGS

1 pound sweet potatoes (about 2 large or 3 medium), grated on large side of box grater or food processor

2 tbsp coconut oil, melted

9 eggs (or 8 eggs + 2 egg whites), divided

Sea salt and fresh-cracked pepper to taste

¼ cup almond milk

2 Roma tomatoes (½ cup), diced

6 strips thick-cut bacon, cooked and diced

2½ oz fresh spinach, chopped

2 tbsp chopped fresh herbs (such as basil, oregano, and chives)

1. Preheat oven to 400°F. Grease a 9-inch pie plate (glass works very well). In a large bowl, mix the grated sweet potatoes, coconut oil, 1 egg (or 2 whites), and salt and pepper to taste. Press into the pie plate and bake for 35 minutes or until slightly golden and crispy on the upper edges. Remove from oven and set aside.

2. In a separate bowl, whisk the 8 remaining eggs, sea salt, pepper, and almond milk.

3. Stir in the tomatoes, bacon, spinach, and fresh herbs, pour over crust, and return to oven.

4. Turn oven down to 375°F and cook for 40 to 45 minutes or until most of the egg is set and firm and just the center is a bit jiggly, but not wet to the touch. Remove from oven and allow to stand 30 minutes. Serve.

Bacon and Sweet Potato Meatballs   *Good - Moist*

Meatballs are a family favorite, if not for their great taste and simplicity then for the ease with which little kids can eat them. When these meatballs are cool enough, my kids will eat them like apples. The bacon lends a salty complexity while the sweet potatoes give the meatballs a softer texture and of course they add a touch of sweetness. These are great for breakfast if prepared the night before, for snacks at games and on road trips, or simply paired with steamed vegetables for a quick dinner. This recipe calls for steaming the cut and peeled sweet potatoes (instead of boiling), which keeps the potatoes from being overly moist before mixing them into the meat. Alternatively, you could bake whole potatoes at 400°F for approximately 45 minutes (or until soft) and then scrape out the insides.

YIELD: 4–6 SERVINGS

① "browned" under broiler parchment lined jelly roll turned over once

① baked on 375° in 9×13 pans after browning for 18 min

1 pound sweet potatoes, peeled and roughly chopped

2 pounds mixed ground meat (pastured pork, bison, turkey, etc.) *I used 3 – 2 beef 1 pork*

12 oz thick-cut bacon, finely chopped *could use less 8g*

1 clove garlic, minced

2 tsp dried oregano

1 tbsp Dijon mustard

1 tbsp coconut aminos or gluten-free soy sauce

2 pastured eggs

¼ cup arrowroot flour

2 tbsp coconut flour

¼ cup coconut oil

1 tsp Sea Salt
½ tsp Pepper

1. Steam potatoes 20 to 25 minutes. While they are still hot, mash with a potato masher or immersion blender until smooth and set aside to cool.

2. Once cool, mix the potatoes, ground meat, bacon, garlic, oregano, Dijon, coconut aminos or soy sauce, and eggs until combined. Once combined, add in the arrowroot and coconut flours.

3. Roll into golf ball–sized balls and refrigerate for 2 hours to firm up.

4. Preheat oven to 400°F. In a large, heavy sauté pan on medium-high heat, heat coconut oil until very hot. Sear balls on all sides and transfer to a baking tray in preheated oven. Finish balls in oven for 10 to 15 minutes and serve.

Baked Salmon with Blueberry Sauce

Living in the Pacific Northwest my whole life has lent me a certain taste for seafood, especially salmon. Then again it could have been the fact that my mother was a very talented salmon fishing guide. In any case, I can never have enough salmon, especially in late summer when the sockeye run. Sockeye has a very red flesh that is lower in fat than some other types of salmon and makes for a perfect grilling fish. It may seem odd, at first, to pair salmon with blueberries, but once you try this combination, you won't doubt it for a second.

YIELD: 6–8 SERVINGS

For the Salmon

1 large wild salmon fillet, skin on

2 tbsp coconut oil

Sea salt and fresh-cracked pepper to taste

For the Blueberry Sauce

1½ cups frozen blueberries (fresh is fine in season too)

¼ cup aged balsamic vinegar

Juice and zest of 1 lemon

1 tsp fresh thyme, minced

½ cup coconut milk

½ cup water

1 tsp pure vanilla extract

¼ cup coconut oil

1 tbsp arrowroot flour + 2 tbsp water (optional)

Sea salt and fresh-cracked pepper to taste

1. Prepare the salmon: Preheat oven to 400°F and line a baking tray with foil or set an outdoor grill to medium high and cover grill with aluminum foil. In a small bowl, mix coconut oil, salt, and pepper. Brush over salmon fillet, and let marinate.

2. Make the sauce: In a small saucepan, place the blueberries, vinegar, lemon zest and juice, thyme, coconut milk, water, and vanilla extract. Bring to a boil and then reduce to a simmer. Continue to simmer for 25 to 30 minutes or until sauce reduces by half. Add in the coconut oil and cook 5 more minutes. If sauce is not thick enough, mix the arrowroot flour with 2 tbsp water and add to sauce. Bring back to a boil and cook 1 to 2 minutes. Season with sea salt and pepper if desired.

3. While sauce is cooking, place the salmon fillet in the oven or on the grill and cook 20 to 30 minutes or until just cooked. (Test by pressing on the middle of the thickest part. It should be firm but not hard and not squishy. If the juices have turned white it is most definitely very done, but preferably you should remove from the heat before all the juices turn white.)

4. Pour sauce over salmon and serve.

Creamy Almond Butter Pork "Pad Thai"

This is a take on both pad thai and peanut satay, making a very rich, creamy, and umami-filled dish. The sauce itself is quite filling, so serving it on delicious, healthy, and low-calorie zucchini noodles only makes sense! Have everything prepped and ready to go before you begin, to make the whole process a lot smoother.

YIELD: 4 SERVINGS

For the Almond Butter Sauce

2 tbsp fish sauce

1 tbsp coconut aminos or gluten-free soy sauce

½ cup homemade or low-sodium chicken stock

1 cup coconut milk

1 tbsp fresh ginger, grated

1 clove garlic, minced or grated

Juice of 2 Key limes or ½ regular lime

½ tsp chili flakes

½ cup smooth almond butter

For the Pork and Noodles

2 tbsp coconut oil

1 sweet onion, sliced into half moons

2 pounds pork, sliced (any cut will work—loin, shoulder, butt, etc.)

2 pounds zucchini, grated, spiral-sliced, or sliced on a mandoline into noodles

1. Make the sauce: In a small bowl mix the fish sauce, aminos or soy sauce, stock, coconut milk, ginger, garlic, lime juice, and chili flakes. Into a separate, larger bowl, pour the almond butter. Slowly mix the fish sauce mixture into the almond butter until completely combined. Set aside.

2. Make the pork and noodles: In a heavy frying pan on medium-high heat, melt the coconut oil. When it's hot, add the onions and sauté for 10 minutes, or until golden and soft. Add the pork and cook thoroughly. Toss in the zucchini noodles and cook for a few minutes. If there looks to be a lot of liquid, drain it off.

3. Pour the almond butter sauce over everything and heat to a good temperature (I like my food molten-lava hot). Portion out and serve immediately. Garnish with chili flakes, cilantro, or chopped almonds if desired.

Pork Chops and Apple Compote

Applesauce and pork chops go back a long time, as far back as the Romans, who ate a dish called *minutal matianum*, a ragout of pork containing apples. It was said that the acidity of apples helped the digestion of the fatty meat of pork. Sadly, I was never a fan of the runny sauce with my pork chops. Instead, I created a sort of quick jam or compote. The chunky consistency, mixed with the acidity of the apples and lemon, makes for a beautiful companion to a freshly grilled or fried chunk of pastured pork.

YIELD: 4 SERVINGS

Apple Compote

1 small sweet onion, or ½ large onion, peeled and diced very finely

2 small tart apples (such as Pink Lady), peeled, cored, and diced very finely

1 tbsp coconut oil

1 tbsp honey

¼ tsp cinnamon

¼ tsp nutmeg

Juice and zest of 1 lemon

Pork Chops

2 tbsp coconut oil

Sea salt and fresh-cracked pepper to taste

4 thick-cut pastured pork chops (loin or rib end)

1. Make the compote: In a small saucepan, combine all compote ingredients and set over medium heat.

2. Cook, stirring occasionally, 35 to 45 minutes, or until a sauce-like consistency is reached and apples and onions are soft.

3. Meanwhile, make the pork chops: Preheat the oven to 400°F and place a heavy baking tray in the middle rack. In a heavy, cast-iron pan, melt the coconut oil over medium-high heat.

4. Season the chops on all sides with salt and pepper. Place in hot pan and sear for 3 to 4 minutes per side. Transfer to oven and allow to cook for approximately 10 minutes or until a thermometer inserted into thickest part of chop reads 145°F.

5. Serve compote over pork chops.

led Pork and Sugar-Free BBQ Sauce

When I went Paleo, I reveled in all the new kinds of meat I was willing to try. The only thing that took getting used to were the ingredients I could use to flavor and enhance all this wonderful protein. Summer pulled-pork barbecues were a staple every year, but I couldn't use those sugar-laden barbecue sauces. I had to relearn the art of barbecue, but once I did, I could never go back. This recipe uses no sugar and relies on the simple ingredients to lend sweetness to the sauce.

YIELD: 6–8 SERVINGS WITH EXTRA SAUCE

For the Pork

1 tbsp coconut oil

4–5-pound pork leg roast (boneless and skinless)

Sea salt and fresh-cracked pepper to taste

1 onion, sliced into half moons (optional)

2 cups low-sodium broth (beef, pork, or chicken)

For the BBQ Sauce

2 tbsp coconut oil

1 large sweet onion, chopped

14-oz can diced tomatoes (no salt added)

¼ cup aged balsamic vinegar (do not use regular)

1 tbsp Dijon mustard

1 clove garlic, minced or grated

2 tsp smoked paprika

½ tsp sea salt

1 tsp liquid smoke

1 tsp chipotle in adobo sauce, minced (optional)

1 tsp instant coffee granules

1. Make the pork: In a heavy-duty frying pan (cast iron works best), heat the coconut oil over medium-high heat. Sear the pork on all sides and season with salt and pepper. Remove from pan and set aside.

2. Place the sliced onions (if using) in the bottom of a slow cooker. Place the seared roast on top of the onions (or into the empty slow cooker if not using onions), pour broth over, and season again with salt and pepper. Set cooker to low and cook 8 hours.

3. Meanwhile, make the sauce: In a large saucepan, heat coconut oil over medium-high heat. Add onions and cook, stirring occasionally, for 10 to 15 minutes or until onions are golden in color and caramelized. Add remaining ingredients and blend with an immersion blender until smooth. Bring to a boil, immediately lower to a simmer, and continue to cook 1 hour or until sauce reduces by at least half. Keep a lid on the saucepan, but make sure it is askew slightly, which allows the steam to escape and the sauce to reduce but keeps messy splatter from getting everywhere.

4. When roast is done, remove from slow cooker and shred using two forks to pull the meat apart. Mix the pulled pork with Sugar-Free BBQ Sauce and ¼ cup of the liquid from the slow cooker, if desired.

Primal Burgers

Burgers are a summer staple for most North Americans. BBQs and backyard parties thrive on simple foods like these and they are quick and easy to prepare in advance. The only problem arises out of those fluffy, white buns served at most of these gatherings. Being grain-free can sometimes pose problems at group events but with these burgers, everyone is happy. Choosing the right lettuce for your burger wrap is key. The best varieties are iceberg and butter lettuce, as they have wide, sturdy leaves to support all the toppings. For best results use 50 percent ground pork for a juicy patty.

YIELD: 6–8 PATTIES

2 tsp + 1 tbsp coconut oil

1 clove garlic, minced

½ sweet onion, finely diced

2 pounds mixed ground meat (pork, beef, elk, lamb, etc.)

2 tsp mesquite liquid smoke

2 tsp dried basil

1 tsp sea salt

6–8 lettuce leaves for wrapping (butter or iceberg)

Toppings

Pico de gallo (page 67)

Sliced fresh tomatoes

Guacamole or sliced fresh avocado

Bacon

Sauteed mushrooms

1. In a heavy cast-iron pan (or other heavy pan), heat the 2 tsp of coconut oil over medium-high heat. Add the garlic and onion and cook until golden brown and caramelized (10 to 15 minutes). Set aside to cool.

2. While the onions cool, mix the ground meat with the liquid smoke, dried basil and salt. Add in the onions and garlic when cool enough to handle. Combine everything until well mixed.

3. Form patties by hand or with a patty press (about 4 to 6 oz each). Preheat oven to 425°F or prepare your outdoor grill as per manufacturer's instructions.

4. Grease a heavy-duty baking pan with a small amount of coconut oil (just enough to coat) and place the formed patties on to it (omit this step if using an outdoor grill). Drizzle remaining coconut oil over the patties.

5. Cook patties in preheated oven for 10 to 15 minutes. Set oven to broil and cook for 1 to 2 minutes. On a grill, cook patties for about 4 to 5 minutes per side on medium-high heat.

6. Wrap each patty in a lettuce leaf with pico de gallo and other toppings listed above, and serve.

Primal Chili

This recipe makes a huge pot of chili and is one of my favorite meals when it starts to get cold outside. I start mine in the morning and cook it all day on the stove. Not only does the house smell fantastic, but I can get anything I need done throughout the day while it cooks to a meaty perfection all by itself. Alternatively, you can cook this in a slow cooker on low for 8 hours, but make sure to brown everything in a pan before adding to the slow cooker for best flavor.

YIELD: 6–8 SERVINGS

2 tbsp coconut oil

3 cloves garlic, peeled and minced or grated

1 large sweet onion, peeled and diced

½ pound mushrooms, sliced

½ pound (250 grams) ground grass-fed sirloin or extra-lean ground beef

½ pound (250 grams) ground pastured pork

2 stalks celery (and leaves), chopped

2 small zucchini, sliced into half moons

2 small sweet bell peppers (yellow, orange, or red), diced

28-oz can diced tomatoes (no salt added)

2–3 sundried tomatoes, finely diced

2 tbsp tomato paste (no sugar added)

1–2 tbsp chili powder

1 tsp ground cumin

1 tsp dried oregano

½ tsp ground coriander

2 tsp porcini mushroom powder, or dried mushrooms ground up fine (optional but optimal!)

1 tbsp coconut aminos

Sea salt and fresh-cracked pepper to taste

5 large kale leaves, stems removed and leaves chopped

¼ cup fresh cilantro, minced

Sliced avocados, for garnish

1. In a large pot, melt the oil over medium-high heat. Add in the garlic, onions, and mushrooms. Brown them completely before removing them from the pot and setting aside in a large bowl.

2. Keeping the heat where it is, add in the ground meat and evenly brown it. This should take about 5 to 7 minutes. Once the meat is brown, add the vegetables back into the pot.

3. Add the celery, zucchini, and peppers into the pot, along with the canned tomatoes, sundried tomatoes, and tomato paste.

4. Finally, add in the seasonings (chili, cumin, oregano, coriander, mushroom powder, and aminos) and season to taste with salt and pepper. Cook, on a low simmer, until the vegetables are softened (I like to cook my chili for a minimum of 4 hours). When it's done, add in the kale and cilantro and cook for an additional 4 to 5 minutes.

5. Serve with sliced avocados on top for a cooling and creamy treat.

Note: Other delicious vegetable additions are fresh, chopped okra (a great natural thickener) and a drier squash, such as Cutie Pie or Kabocha, in large cubes.

Beef Stew

Nothing is quite as comforting on a cold, wintry day as a steaming-hot bowl of beef stew. Filling, nutritious, and easy to prepare, this stew is versatile and can take on many shapes depending on what vegetables are added. The longer you simmer this stew, the softer the meat and vegetables become. Using the cheap and lean cuts makes for the most flavorful dish. I like to use hip, chuck, bottom or top round, pot roast, or rump.

YIELD: 6–8 SERVINGS

2 tbsp coconut oil

1½ pounds grass-fed beef or bison, cubed
   (choose a leaner cut if possible)

2 small or 1 large leek, halved lengthwise
   and sliced thin

1 bunch celery (8–10 stalks), chopped

½ pound carrots, peeled and chopped

2 tsp Dijon mustard

2 tsp dried herbs, such as rosemary, thyme,
   oregano (or use fresh in same quantities)

1 tbsp coconut aminos or gluten-free soy sauce

6–8 cups homemade beef stock (or organic,
   low sodium)

Optional Add-ins (use 2 cups total or less)

Butternut squash, peeled, seeded, and cubed

Rutabaga, peeled and cubed

Potatoes, peeled and cubed

Kale or spinach, chopped

1. In a heavy-duty pan, heat the coconut oil over medium-high heat. Sear the beef or bison until browned and toss into a Dutch oven or heavy-duty pot.

2. Sear the vegetables in the same frying pan (without cleaning it out) until slightly browned and softened. Add to the meat in the Dutch oven.

3. Stir the Dijon, herbs, and aminos or soy sauce into the meat and vegetables. Pour in the stock and set the Dutch oven or pot over medium-high heat until it comes to a slight boil. Turn the heat down to low and allow to simmer for 2 to 4 hours. Add in the optional vegetables during the simmering phase for maximum tenderness. If using kale or spinach, add it about 10 minutes before serving.

4. Serve hot.

w-Cooker Short Ribs

Short ribs are an underutilized cut of beef, often overcooked or mistreated with various sugar-laden sauces. Because short ribs contain bones and connective tissues, they are rich in gelatin (a good source of protein) and create their own deliciously rich gravy when braised. Keeping the braising liquid simple makes the resulting dish rich, beefy, and quite filling. Make sure to use grass-fed/finished beef for the highest quality protein possible.

YIELD: 6 SERVINGS

2 tbsp coconut oil

2–3 pounds Korean-style short ribs

Sea salt and fresh-cracked pepper to taste

3 tbsp coconut aminos or gluten-free soy sauce

2 tbsp aged balsamic vinegar

1 tbsp Dijon mustard

1 clove garlic, minced very finely or grated

2 tsp instant coffee granules

¼ cup hot water (you can replace the instant coffee granules and water with ¼ cup brewed espresso or very strong coffee)

2 tbsp coconut oil, melted

1. Heat a heavy frying pan over medium-high heat. Add coconut oil and allow it to get very hot. When you put the ribs in, the oil should spit and crackle a bit. Sear ribs on all sides, seasoning with salt and pepper to taste. Place ribs in a slow cooker.

2. In a small bowl, mix the aminos (or soy sauce), balsamic vinegar, Dijon, garlic, coffee and water, and oil. Pour the sauce over the ribs and set the slow cooker to low. Cook for 8 hours.

3. Serve.

Bison and Kale Wraps

Wrapping up food and rolling it into shapes convenient enough to carry to our mouths can be a fun adventure, one everyone (even grain- and gluten-free eaters) should enjoy. There's just something extremely primal about eating your food with your hands. Large leaves of dinosaur (lacinato) kale make for the best rolls, but any kale with large enough leaves will do just fine in this recipe. These are great dipped in creamy aioli and served with a side salad!

YIELD: 3–6 SERVINGS

6 large kale leaves

2 tsp coconut oil

1 small onion, diced

1 clove garlic, minced or grated

¾ cup shredded carrot (2–3 medium carrots)

2 cups shredded zucchini (about 3 medium
    zucchinis), squeezed of excess moisture

2 cups shredded green cabbage (about ⅓ head)

1 pound (about 500 grams) extra-lean grass-fed
    ground beef or bison (or a mixture of the two)

Sea salt and fresh-cracked pepper to taste

2 tbsp coconut aminos or gluten-free soy sauce

¼ tsp cayenne

1½ tsp dried oregano

¼ tsp coriander

1 tsp chili powder

½ cup chopped tomatoes (optional garnish)

½ avocado, sliced (optional garnish)

¼ cup chopped chives (optional garnish)

1. Cut the stems off the kale at the bottom of the leaf. Flip the kale over and run the knife parallel to the leaf, removing the tough stem but not cutting through the leaf, to make it flatter. This will also make it easier to bite into it.

2. Fill a pot fitted with a steamer basket with 2 inches of water. Bring to a boil and arrange leaves flat in the steamer. Steam for about 3 minutes. Remove and drain on towels. Set aside until needed.

3. In a heavy saucepan (cast iron is best) on medium-high heat, heat coconut oil. Place the onion and garlic in the pan and cook for about 5 minutes or until onions are browned. Add in the other vegetables and cook until softened.

4. Add in the ground meat and cook for another 7 to 8 minutes, or until browned. Season with salt, pepper, coconut aminos or soy sauce, and spices. Remove from heat.

5. Place a large spoonful of the meat mixture onto a flattened and laid-out kale leaf. Top with optional garnishes. Roll the bottom of the leaf over the meat, then each side into the middle, and finally roll up like a burrito. Set seam side down on plates and serve.

Spaghetti Squash Bolognese

A simple family favorite, like spaghetti and meat sauce, was something I sorely missed after leaving home. We used to sit down to that meal on a regular basis when I was a kid, complete with a big loaf of garlic bread and grated cheese to top it off. Now that I have my own family, I wanted to make this old tradition part of our lives as well but in a more flavorful and healthy way. This is my absolute favorite way to serve spaghetti squash and even my littlest eater enjoys slurping up the "noodles."

YIELD: 4 SERVINGS

2 tbsp coconut oil

2–3 pounds ground meat (grass-fed bison or beef, turkey, chicken, etc. At least 50 percent should be pastured pork)

Sea salt and fresh-cracked pepper to taste

½ pound mushrooms, sliced

1 large onion, diced

1 clove garlic

1 tsp each dried oregano, marjoram, and basil

½ tsp instant coffee granules

½ tsp ground cinnamon

1 (14-oz) can diced tomatoes (no salt added)

1 (28-oz) can crushed tomatoes (no salt added)

1 large or 2 small spaghetti squash (about 2 pounds), cut in half, seeds removed

2 tsp coconut oil, melted

1. In a large sauté pan on medium heat, heat the coconut oil and brown the ground meats. Season to taste with salt and pepper and transfer to a large pot, slow cooker, or Dutch oven.

2. In the same pan on medium heat, sauté the mushrooms, onion, and garlic until browned and transfer to the pot with the meat in it.

3. Add the herbs, coffee, cinnamon, and tomatoes into the pot, stir, and set on medium heat until it begins to bubble. Turn down to low and allow to simmer for 2 to 4 hours (up to 8 hours in a slow cooker).

4. An hour before dinner-time, preheat the oven to 425°F. Brush the squash with the melted coconut oil and place cut side down on a greased baking pan. Bake in the preheated oven for 45 minutes. When done, scrape a fork along the sides of the squash to make the spaghetti "noodles," then scoop out into serving dishes. Top with Bolognese sauce and serve.

Grilled Skirt Steak with Chimichurri

Chimichurri originates in Argentina and its name has a rich and diverse history. Some say it came from Argentinean natives not being able to pronounce the name of the original creator, "Jimmy Curry" or "Jimmy McCurry." Some other stories also say it could have been a rough translation of a Basque term simply meaning "a mixture of several things in no particular order." The fun of chimichurri is that anything goes, really. If you don't like cilantro, replace it with more parsley. Some variations include paprika, thyme, bay leaf, or tomato. This version is especially bright and tangy and pairs extremely well with the skirt steak but also works with just about any grilled meat.

YIELD: 2–4 SERVINGS, 1 ½ CUPS CHIMICHURRI

For the Chimichurri

1 cup fresh Italian flat leaf parsley, packed

1 cup fresh cilantro, packed

¼ cup fresh oregano, packed

¼ cup fresh basil, packed

4 green onions or scallions, green part only

1 clove garlic, peeled

Juice of 1 lemon at room temperature

¼ cup coconut oil, melted

1 tbsp red wine vinegar

Sea salt and fresh-cracked pepper to taste

½ tsp red pepper flakes

For the Steak

2 tbsp coconut oil, melted

1 skirt steak (approximately ¾ to 1 pound)

Sea salt and fresh-cracked pepper to taste

1. Make the chimichurri: Place everything in a food processor or blender and blend until smooth. Set aside if you're cooking the steak immediately, or keep covered in the fridge. Bring to room temperature before using.

2. Heat grill on high.

3. Brush coconut oil over skirt steak and season with salt and pepper.

4. Place on grill. Sear steak for 3 to 4 minutes per side for medium rare, 5 to 7 minutes for well done.

5. Remove from grill and slice against the grain of the meat. Place slices on plates or on a platter, spoon chimichurri over, and serve immediately.

Braised Lamb Shanks

Tough cuts of meat are often overlooked by the average shopper simply because they aren't sure how to cook them. Shanks, cheeks, oxtail, short ribs—these are all wonderful, flavorful, and economical cuts of meat that require just a little forethought to create wonderful, restaurant-quality meals. They don't take any more effort (less, even!) than your average dinner, but you must plan ahead to make them because most require long hours of braising to reach their full potential.

YIELD: 2–4 SERVINGS

2 tbsp coconut oil

2–3 lamb shanks

Sea salt and fresh-cracked pepper to taste

2 cloves garlic, peeled

1 large sweet onion, halved and sliced into half
   moons

⅓ cup water or sodium-free stock

1 tbsp Dijon mustard

2 tbsp aged balsamic vinegar

2 tsp coconut aminos

2 sprigs fresh rosemary

1. In a heavy-bottomed saucepan on medium-high heat, melt 1 tbsp of coconut oil until very hot.

2. Sear each lamb shank on all sides and season with salt and pepper. Place in the crock of a slow cooker and set aside.

3. Heat remaining oil in same pan and sauté garlic and onions until slightly browned. Add these to the slow cooker. Deglaze the pan with the stock or water and pour over the shanks.

4. In a small bowl, whisk the Dijon, balsamic vinegar, and aminos into a sauce. Pour the sauce over the shanks, place the rosemary on top of everything, and set the slow cooker to low. Cook for 8 hours.

5. Remove the rosemary from the slow cooker, transfer to platter or plates, and serve.

Snacks and Starters

Avocado and Shrimp Canapés on Endive Boats

Although endive is not available year-round and most people have never used it, it does make quite a statement when used for appetizers. Two small heads of endive will make this whole recipe! The flavor is sweet, with a slight bitter aftertaste that marries well with the smooth avocado and bright notes of the mango and citrus. It also adds a nice little crunch to the soft mixture inside, especially when paired with some crisp bacon crumbles. This recipe calls for ataulfo mangoes, a small yellow variety grown in Mexico with a high sugar content, a small, thin pit, and little to no fibrousness. In a pinch, any mango will do.

YIELD: 2–4 SERVINGS

2 heads broad-leaf endive (not the frisée kind)

1 ataulfo mango

1 large Hass avocado

12 large shrimp, cooked and roughly chopped
    or 150 g pink (or cold water) shrimp, cooked

1 tsp Dijon mustard

2 tbsp coconut oil, melted

Juice and zest of 1 lime

2 tbsp red wine vinegar

Sea salt and fresh-cracked pepper to taste

2 slices thick-cut bacon, cooked crisp and
    crumbled (optional)

1. Separate the leaves of the endive and place on a platter or serving dish.

2. Peel, pit, and dice both the mango and the avocado. Mix with the shrimp in a medium bowl.

3. Make the dressing: In a small bowl, add the Dijon mustard. Whisk in the coconut oil until smooth, then add the lime juice and zest. Add the red wine vinegar, salt, and pepper to the dressing and mix with the mango, avocado, and shrimp.

4. Scoop the mixture into the endive boats and top with the optional bacon garnish. Serve immediately. (Because of the nature of coconut oil to harden at lower temperatures, this dish is best made and served immediately.)

Avocado Mousse in Cucumber Cups

In this age of multiple food allergies and sensitivities, making appetizers that you can bring anywhere can be tough. These little canapés are super easy and quick to make, plus they look and taste like you slaved for hours over them! They are perfect for summer gatherings and make great bases for other toppers such as shrimp, prawns, herbs, chunks of fresh mango, or fresh peels of lime or lemon. The possibilities are endless! Make up to two hours ahead for best taste and appearance.

YIELD: 20+ APPETIZER SERVINGS

2 cups water, room temperature (optional)

¼ cup sea salt (optional)

1 large avocado, room temperature

1 long English cucumber, cut into rounds about
   ¾ inch thick

Juice and zest of 1 Key lime or ½ regular lime

2 tbsp coconut oil, melted

Handful fresh chives, minced, plus more for garnish

Sea salt and fresh-cracked pepper to taste

1. Place water in a bowl and stir in ¼ cup sea salt. Peel and remove the pit from the avocado and place the flesh in the bowl of water. Allow it to sit for 5 minutes and then drain it. (This step is optional but makes sure the avocado stays green if you are not using the canapés right away.)

2. Using a melon baller or spoon, scoop out most of the flesh of each cucumber round, leaving a small amount at the bottom to form little bowls.

3. In the bowl of a food processor, place the avocado and lime. Blend until smooth. Slowly pour in the coconut oil until completely blended, then mix in the chives and salt and pepper to taste. Blend again to mix.

4. Place the avocado mixture in a piping bag fitted with a tip that has a large opening, and pipe the avocado mixture into the cucumber rounds. Garnish with more chives or other desired toppings and serve. (You can also just use a small spoon to carefully scoop the avocado mixture into the cucumbers.)

5. If not using right away, either keep the ingredients separate and pipe the avocado just before serving, or assemble it all beforehand and keep wrapped tightly in plastic film.

Crispy Chicken Wings with Preserved Lemon Aioli

There's nothing like chicken wings, those crispy, salty, soul-satisfying snacks. Sadly, most restaurants douse theirs in white flour or cornstarch and deep-fry them in heavily used vegetable oils. These wings, on the other hand, use flour made from arrowroot, a starchy tuber, and are fried in the delicious and heart-healthy oil for which this book is named.

YIELD: 4 SERVINGS

For the Preserved Lemon Aioli

½ cup coconut oil mayonnaise

1 tsp Dijon mustard

3 tbsp almond milk

1 clove garlic, minced or grated

Sea salt and fresh-cracked pepper to taste

2 tsp preserved lemon rind, minced finely

For the Chicken Wings

2 pounds chicken wings

½–¾ cup arrowroot flour

Sea salt and fresh-cracked pepper to taste

1 cup coconut oil

1. Make Preserved Lemon Aioli: Mix all ingredients until combined. Set aside; refrigerate if not using immediately.

2. With a sharp knife, separate chicken drumettes from wing tips.

3. On a large plate or in a shallow bowl, place the flour, salt, and pepper and stir to combine.

4. Melt the coconut oil in a medium saucepan on medium-high heat. Preheat the oven to 425°F and set a wire baking rack over a solid baking pan and place in the oven (just a solid sheet pan will work as well).

5. Coat the wings with the flour mixture and fry a few at a time in the heated oil for 1 minute per side. Once crispy and slightly golden brown, transfer to sheet in oven.

6. Continue steps until all wings are in the oven. Bake wings for a total of 10 to 15 minutes after frying. Serve hot with Preserved Lemon Aioli for dipping.

Note: Preserved lemon can be found in many import and specialty food shops. It comes in jars and can last for months.

Deviled Guacamole Eggs

Deviled eggs are often seen as a throwback appetizer, a bit of an old-school thing to bring to a party. With the advent of low-carb, Paleo, gluten-free, and other grain-free diets as well as the new research showing that cholesterol and saturated fats aren't the nutritional demons they have been made out to be, these guys will be the next big thing in no time! My biggest problem with deviled eggs has always been that they are very rich. This recipe solves that problem by cutting the richness with the fresh notes of lime and mixing the yolks with avocado. They are still rich and velvety, but it's much easier to eat too many of them when they are like a fiesta in your mouth! This recipe calls for steaming the eggs, which makes peeling them quicker, but boiling them directly in water works too.

YIELD: 16 PIECES

8 pastured eggs, room temperature

½ large avocado

Juice of ½ lime

1 tbsp coconut oil, room temperature

Dash of hot sauce (optional)

½ Roma tomato or 3 small cherry tomatoes, minced

1 tbsp fresh cilantro, minced

Sea salt and fresh-cracked pepper to taste

1. Fill a large pot (that has a steamer attachment) with 3 inches of water. Bring the water to a boil over high heat. Place the eggs in the steamer attachment and set over the boiling water for 12 minutes. Alternatively, you can boil them the old-fashioned way by setting the eggs directly in boiling water for 12 minutes. Immediately plunge the eggs into ice-cold water and cool completely.

2. Peel the cooled eggs and then cut in half. Put the yolks into the bowl of a food processor or blender, or a bowl. Set the whites aside until the last step.

3. Add the avocado, lime juice, coconut oil, and hot sauce (if using) to the yolks, and either pulse until smooth or mash with a fork. Stir in the minced tomatoes and cilantro, and season with salt and pepper.

4. Scoop the filling into the whites, garnish with more minced cilantro (or paprika if you want to be old-school), and serve. If serving later, wrap completely in plastic and keep in the refrigerator.

Lemon-Cashew Dip

This dip is zesty, garlicky, and makes a perfect accompaniment to crisp vegetables or chips. The key to a smooth dip is to blend the cashews until they are absolutely smooth. In a blender or a food processor, this means you must take the time to scrape down the sides a lot as you blend. If you can't find nutritional yeast (it's available at most health food stores or grocery stores with a bulk section), either leave it out or replace with a tablespoon of very sharp Parmesan cheese.

YIELD: 2 CUPS

1 cup raw cashews

2 tbsp coconut oil

Zest and juice of 1 lemon

1 tbsp nutritional yeast

¼ tsp sea salt

1 clove garlic, minced

1. Fill a bowl with 2 to 3 cups of cold, filtered water. Place the cashews in the water and refrigerate overnight or for a minimum of 4 hours. Drain the nuts and place them in the bowl of a food processor or blender.

2. Add remaining ingredients and blend on high speed until smooth. Scrape down the sides often.

3. Serve immediately with fresh vegetables or chips. Because of the nature of coconut oil, this dip hardens quite a bit when refrigerated. If there are leftovers, simply remove from the fridge 30 minutes prior to serving for best results.

Roasted Beet and Cauliflower Hummus

Roasting beets brings out a natural sweetness in them that lends itself well to many uses in sweet and savory dishes. Roasting them with the skin on ensures that they don't dry out too much, which is especially helpful when you are going to blend them up into a dip. The same goes for cauliflower. Though not many people roast their cauliflower, it does create a certain sweetness in this cruciferous vegetable that makes a unique and interesting flavor mixed with the beets. The best part about this dip, though, is its vibrant pink hue. Serve with bright green cucumber slices, yellow spears of pepper, or wedges of Coconut-Flour Sopes (found on page 67).

YIELD: APPROXIMATELY 2 CUPS

4 small beets, skin on and tops and bottoms removed

About ½ an average-size head of cauliflower (225 g), cut into florets

1 tbsp coconut oil, melted

Juice of 1 lemon

2 tbsp tahini

Sea salt and fresh-cracked pepper to taste

1 clove garlic, minced

1. Preheat oven to 400°F. Place beets in a shallow baking dish and bake, uncovered, for 35 to 40 minutes.

2. Toss cauliflower with the coconut oil and pour into a separate shallow baking dish. Place in oven and bake, uncovered, for 25 minutes.

3. When both vegetables are done, slip the skins off the beets, and place beets and cauliflower in a food processor with remaining ingredients. Blend on medium speed, scraping the sides down occasionally, until smooth. Serve immediately or keep in fridge, covered, until needed.

Scotch Eggs

Unless you are Scottish, a member of a Scottish marching band, a bagpiper, or a big fan of Scottish food, you may never have heard of Scotch eggs. I've heard them called an acquired taste, although I don't find them to be anything but delicious. Hard-boiled eggs wrapped in sausage? It's just breakfast in a neat little package. Traditional Scotch eggs have a final step not added here: They are breaded and then deep-fried. If you ask me, though, they are just fine without any coating whatsoever and are best served immediately and with a little Dijon mustard for dipping.

YIELD: 8 PIECES

9 pastured eggs, room temperature

2 pounds ground pork or sausage meat

1 tbsp dried spices and herbs (such as basil, oregano, cumin, garlic, mace, sage, fennel, or coriander)

Sea salt and fresh-cracked pepper

2 tbsp coconut oil

1. Fill a large pot (that has a steamer attachment) with 3 inches of water. Bring the water to a boil over high heat. Place 8 of the eggs in the steamer attachment and set over the boiling water for 10 minutes. Alternatively, you can boil them the old-fashioned way by setting the eggs directly in boiling water for 10 minutes. Immediately plunge the eggs into ice-cold water and cool completely.

2. Peel the eggs and dry them with a kitchen cloth or paper towel. Set aside.

3. In a large bowl, mix the ground meat with the desired spices and herbs, season with salt and pepper, and then mix in the last egg. Using your hands is the best way to get the spices, seasonings, and egg completely mixed in. Don't be afraid to get your hands dirty!

4. Take a bit of the pork mixture and roll it into a large ball (bigger than a golf ball, but not so big as a tennis ball). Indent the ball with your thumbs and put a hard-boiled egg inside. Keep working the sausage until it is completely wrapped around the egg. You want the sausage layer to be at least ½ inch thick and have no holes. Repeat until all the eggs and sausage are used.

5. Preheat the oven to 400°F. In a large, oven-safe, heavy sauté pan, heat the coconut oil on medium-high heat. Place the Scotch eggs into the hot oil and brown on all sides. When they are golden, move the pan to the hot oven and finish cooking for about 10 to 15 minutes.

6. Remove from oven and serve.

Roasted Butternut Squash Soup

Butternut squash is a favorite for many chefs as it is equally as delicious in savory dishes, like this one, as it is in sweet dishes in place of pumpkin. The dense, moist texture of butternut squash lends itself well to soups, stews, puddings, baked goods, and even salads. Roasting the squash before pureeing ensures that the sweetness of the squash shines through, especially when it is paired with tart apples and creamy coconut. This a wonderfully comforting main dish in the depths of winter, or an easy side to lighter fare.

YIELD: 4 SERVINGS

1 large butternut squash (approximately 2 pounds), peeled, seeds removed

1 large or 2 small (¾ pound total) crisp, tart apples (such as Honeycrisp, Pink Lady, or Granny Smith), peeled and cored

1 small sweet onion

3 stalks celery, leaves on

2 tbsp coconut oil, melted

2 cups homemade or low-sodium chicken or vegetable stock

1 cup full-fat coconut milk

½ tsp ground ginger

½ tsp ground cumin

½ tsp ground coriander

¼ tsp ground cinnamon

⅛ tsp ground nutmeg

2–3 slices thick-cut bacon, diced (optional)

1. Preheat oven to 400°F.

2. Roughly chop the squash, apple, onion, and celery (try to keep the size roughly uniform so that everything cooks in the same time). In a large baking dish, toss vegetables and fruit with the coconut oil and roast in the oven for 40 to 45 minutes.

3. When the fruit and vegetables are done roasting, pour the stock and coconut milk over them and puree with a stick or immersion blender. (You can use a blender or food processor, but putting hot liquids in these appliances can be dangerous.)

4. Add in the spices and blend to combine. Pour the soup into a pot and heat over medium-high heat until it begins to simmer.

5. Cook the bacon, if using, in a hot pan over medium heat until crisp. Crumble it over soup after ladling into bowls or serve on the side.

Chocolate-Coconut Protein Cookie Balls

Making cookies with gluten-free flours is not always an easy task. Lacking the elastic bonding characteristics of gluten and the crisping effects of granulated sugar, most gluten-free cookies end up being soft and flat. Rolling them into balls makes for fun little portion-controlled handheld snacks. My kids love having cookie balls and it makes for more servings in a reasonable size.

YIELD: 15 COOKIE BALLS

½ cup coconut flour

1 (30 g) scoop chocolate protein powder (any kind)

1 tsp gluten-free baking powder

¼ tsp sea salt

½ tsp ground cinnamon

¼ cup mini dark chocolate chips or cacao nibs
   (or a 50-50 mixture of both)

2 tbsp unsweetened shredded coconut

4 medjool dates, pitted and soaked in
   ¼ cup warm water

2 tbsp unsweetened almond milk (or the water
   from soaking the dates)

2 eggs

2 tsp pure vanilla extract

2 tbsp maple syrup

3 tbsp coconut oil, melted

1 tbsp nut butter (cashew, hazelnut, macadamia,
   almond, etc.)

1. Preheat oven to 350°F. Grease a small cookie sheet with coconut oil.

2. In a small bowl, mix the flour, protein powder, baking powder, salt, cinnamon, chocolate chips, and shredded coconut. Set aside.

3. Mash the dates by mincing them and then smashing them with the flat side of a knife until they become a puree, or use a food processor. (If using a blender or food processor, put the soaked dates and the almond milk or date water in the mixer at the same time. Otherwise it won't blend properly.)

4. Continue blending and add the remaining ingredients to the food processor, or whisk vigorously.

5. Pour the wet into the dry and stir together. Allow the batter to sit for a minute (this allows the coconut flour to soak up the moisture, creating a batter dry enough to roll into balls).

6. Make balls roughly the size of golf balls (approximately 2 tbsp of batter) and place on greased cookie sheet.

7. Bake for 12 to 15 minutes or until the bottoms of the cookie balls are golden brown. Remove to cooling rack and cool before storing in an airtight container.

CHOCOLATE
ENERGY
BITES

Chocolate, Fruit, and Nut Energy Bites

Quick little snacks that are calorie dense make great pre-workout snacks or food for on-the-go kids. These little bites are chock-full of antioxidants, fiber, good fats, carbs, and protein. Similar to some very popular prepackaged fruit bars, these guys stand up to anything. I make sure never to leave for a road trip without them. Keep refrigerated for longer storage and a firmer texture.

YIELD: 16 BALLS

6 medjool dates

1½ cups almond meal

½ cup coconut oil

¼ cup almond butter (or other nut butter)

¼ cup maple syrup

2 tsp pure vanilla extract

2 tbsp coconut flour

1 tbsp arrowroot flour

½ tsp sea salt

½ tsp ground cinnamon

¼ cup cocoa powder

¼ cup chopped nuts (pecans, macadamia, cashew, etc.)

1 cup dried fruit (cherries, figs, apricots, etc.), roughly chopped

1. Soak the dates in warm water for 20 minutes to soften them up. Drain, then add them to the bowl of a food processor with the almond meal, coconut oil, almond butter, maple syrup, and vanilla extract. Pulse until smooth and sticky.

2. Add in the remaining ingredients and pulse again until a dough forms.

3. Scrape out into a bowl and roll into small balls (slightly smaller than golf balls) or pat into a greased 8 x 8 pan for cutting into bars. If putting in a smaller container, it's best to put wax or parchment paper between layers to keep them from sticking together.

4. Refrigerate and store up to 1 week.

rbed Crackers

Crackers are a staple for snacks in our house, but there are not a lot of prepackaged varieties that don't contain something I am just not willing to feed my kids. These crackers are delicious on their own or paired with dips, cheese, nut butters, or any other topping you would normally put on a cracker. They stay crisp for days and will keep in an airtight container for up to a week.

YIELD: 2 DOZEN CRACKERS

1 cup + 2 tbsp almond meal

2 tbsp coconut flour

¼ cup golden flax, ground

¼ cup hemp hearts or sesame seeds

¼ cup nutritional yeast

½ tsp sea salt

Fresh-cracked pepper to taste

1 tbsp fresh herbs, minced (rosemary, thyme, oregano, basil, etc.)

1 pastured egg

1 tbsp coconut aminos or gluten-free soy sauce

1 tbsp coconut oil, melted

1. Preheat oven to 375°F. Mix dry ingredients and herbs in a large bowl.

2. In a separate, smaller bowl, whisk the egg and coconut aminos.

3. Pour the coconut oil into the egg mixture and whisk again.

4. Add the wet to the dry and mix together to form a dough. Lay a sheet of parchment paper down and place the dough on it. Lay a second sheet on top and roll out with a rolling pin until just slightly less than ¼ inch thick. Peel the top layer of parchment off, place the bottom piece onto a baking tray (with the dough rolled out on top), slice into cracker shapes with a knife (don't press too hard), and place in the preheated oven for 10 to 12 minutes. After 10 minutes the crackers will be slightly soft and chewy, whereas 12 minutes will yield a crunchier texture.

5. Cool on wire racks and then store in an airtight container.

Desserts
and
Baked Goods

Dark Chocolate Brownies

Brownies are that quintessential chocolate baked good that no one can resist. Whether you are grain-free, nut-free, vegan, diabetic, fruititarian, pescatarian, or have any other special dietary need, there must always be a recipe for brownies that fits your diet. These brownies are free from grains, gluten, dairy, legumes, and refined sugar. They are fudgy and moist and will definitely cure any cravings you have for chocolate goodies.

YIELD: 12–18 BROWNIES

1 cup almond meal

3 tbsp coconut flour

½ tsp sea salt

1 tsp baking powder

½ cup cocoa powder

2 tbsp honey

8 large medjool dates, pitted

1 tbsp pure vanilla extract

2 eggs

½ cup nut butter (such as cashew, hazelnut,
    or almond)

2 oz dark chocolate (70 percent or higher)

⅓ cup coconut oil

1. Preheat oven to 350°F and grease an 8 x 8-inch pan.

2. In a large bowl, blend dry ingredients with a fork. Set aside.

3. In a food processor or high-powered blender, mix the honey, dates, vanilla, eggs, and nut butter until smooth. Set aside.

4. Bring a small pot filled a third of the way with water to a boil, then lower to a simmer and place a small bowl over the water (making certain the bowl is not touching the water) or use a double-boiler for this step. Place the chocolate and coconut oil into the bowl and allow to melt, stirring until combined. Mix this with the wet ingredients.

5. Mix the wet and dry ingredients together and pour into the greased pan. Bake for 22 to 25 minutes. Remove from oven and allow to cool on a cooling rack until they are room temperature. Cut into desired sizes and serve.

Chocolate Brownie Caramel Cups

These cups are pure decadence. Part brownie, part dairy-free caramel, and part dark chocolate ganache, they are every bit amazing. Use the very best dark chocolate you can find and double the recipe if you think you might have to share. Each cup makes a perfect stand-alone dessert.

YIELD: 7 CUPS

For the Brownie Layer

1 cup blanched almond meal

2 tbsp coconut flour

¼ tsp sea salt

½ tsp cinnamon

¼ cup cocoa powder

2 tbsp coconut oil, melted

2 tbsp honey

1 tsp pure vanilla extract

1 pastured egg

For the Caramel Layer

10 large (preferably soft) medjool dates, pitted

3 tbsp boiling water

Slightly less than ¼ tsp sea salt

1 tsp pure vanilla extract

⅓ cup creamed coconut (aka coconut manna, butter, or spread)

For the Chocolate Layer

½ cup (80 g) dark chocolate or chips (70 percent cocoa or higher)

1 tbsp coconut oil

⅛ tsp sea salt

1. For the brownies: Preheat oven to 350°F. Grease a deep silicone muffin pan or line with paper liners, and set aside.

2. In a large bowl, blend almond meal and coconut flour. Add in salt, cinnamon, and cocoa and blend with a fork. Stir in the coconut oil, honey, vanilla, and egg. Blend until completely mixed.

3. Spoon into 6 or 7 of the muffin pan compartments. Bake for 13 to 15 minutes. Remove from oven and cool completely in pan. (For speedier cooling, pop them in the freezer for a few minutes.)

4. For the caramel layer: Place dates and boiling water in a blender or food processor and blend until liquefied. Add in remaining ingredients and blend until smooth. Pour over cooled brownie layer and cool again in the pan.

5. For the chocolate layer: In a double-boiler or a small metal bowl placed over a small pot of gently simmering water, add the chocolate, coconut oil, and salt. Stir continuously until just melted.

6. Pour chocolate over cooled cups and spread around with your finger or a small spatula. Cool completely before trying to remove from cups. Keep in refrigerator for best texture.

Chocolate-Coconut Cake

In our house, when it's someone's birthday, they get to pick whatever cake concoction they can think of. Usually it turns into some iteration of chocolate or vanilla cake with fillings and crazy frosting. This is my all-time favorite cake for parties—it is absolutely perfect (if I do say so myself). The act of separating the eggs and whipping the whites means it's fluffy and light, not overly dense, and chock-a-block full of chocolate goodness. Chocolate cake is always a show stopper, especially when you tell your guests there are no grains, dairy, or refined sugars!

YIELD: 1 (9-INCH) DOUBLE-LAYERED CAKE

¾ cup coconut flour, sifted if lumpy

½ cup arrowroot flour

¾ cup cacao powder (or regular cocoa powder)

1 tsp sea salt

½ tsp cinnamon

2 tsp baking powder

9 pastured eggs, separated

¾ cup coconut oil, melted

½ cup maple syrup

¾ cup brewed strong coffee, cooled

1 tbsp pure vanilla extract

1 tsp cream of tartar

1. Preheat oven to 350°F. Grease two 9-inch baking pans with coconut oil.

2. Sift dry ingredients (except cream of tartar) into a large bowl. Set aside.

3. In a separate bowl, mix egg yolks, coconut oil, maple syrup, coffee, and vanilla with a whisk, hand mixer, or immersion blender.

4. In a large metal bowl, beat the egg whites until foamy. Add in the cream of tartar and beat until stiff peaks form.

5. Mix the dry ingredients into the yolk mixture and then gradually fold in the egg whites.

6. Pour evenly into both greased pans and bake for 25 to 28 minutes, turning halfway if needed. Remove from oven.

7. Cool on baking racks in pans for 10 to 15 minutes, then flip out onto racks and cool completely before frosting with Coconut Frosting (see page 136).

Coconut Frosting

This frosting works well on any flavor of cake—plain Jane vanilla, coconut, chocolate, carrot, fudge, orange, you name it. The three different but similar fats work extremely well together and combine into a beautifully creamy, spreadable, pipeable frosting that mimics a classic buttercream. Use this for frosting and filling cakes, cupcakes, or cookies, as a base for fruit dips, or eat it straight out of the bowl. (Just don't make it a habit!)

YIELD: ENOUGH TO FROST A 2-LAYER 9-INCH CAKE (ABOUT 2½ CUPS)

¾ cup coconut oil, room temperature

¾ cup palm shortening or lard, room temperature

½ cup coconut butter, melted

⅓ cup maple syrup

1 tsp pure vanilla extract

Dash of sea salt

¾ cup coconut flakes or chips (lightly roasted, see note)

1. Blend all ingredients (except coconut flakes) in a stand mixer with paddle attachment or in a bowl with an immersion blender. Blend until smooth.

2. Frost cake as usual, sprinkle with roasted coconut flakes or chips, and store at room temperature for a soft frosting, or in the refrigerator for a harder frosting.

Note: Roast coconut flakes on a light-colored cookie sheet at 300°F for 3 to 4 minutes. Check often to avoid overbrowning.

Carrot Cake

My birthday cake is always carrot cake. I'm not sure when I decided that's what it would be, but I do remember I wanted it for my wedding cake but was turned down by my husband, who didn't think it would go over well with most of the guests. The first thing I thought was: "People don't like carrot cake?!" I think the normal carrot cake, filled with vegetable oil, raisins, walnuts, and other extraneous items, makes some people squeamish. Me, I just take all those things out and call it the best cake ever. This cake freezes very well. Just defrost at room temperature and consume within four days.

YIELD: 1 (9-INCH) DOUBLE-LAYERED CAKE

1 cup almond meal

⅓ cup coconut flour, sifted if lumpy

1 cup arrowroot flour

1 tsp sea salt

2 tsp ground cinnamon

½ tsp ground nutmeg

¾ tsp ground ginger or 1-inch knob fresh ginger, peeled and grated, (if using fresh, add to carrots during recipe)

¼ tsp ground cardamom

2 tsp baking soda

1 tsp corn-free, gluten-free baking powder

9 pastured eggs

½ cup maple syrup

1½ tsp liquid stevia

¾ cup coconut oil or clarified butter, melted

1 tbsp pure vanilla extract

Zest from 1 navel orange

3 cups finely grated carrot

1. Preheat oven to 350°F. Grease two 9-inch baking pans and line with parchment circles.

2. In a large bowl, combine all dry ingredients.

3. In a separate large bowl, combine all wet ingredients (except the carrots and fresh ginger, if using).

4. Pour the dry into the wet ingredients, mixing well. Then stir in the carrots and fresh ginger (if using).

5. Measure batter out equally between pans (I weigh them on a kitchen scale) and then pop them in the preheated oven for 30 to 35 minutes.

6. Remove from oven and cool on cooling rack in pans for 10 to 15 minutes. Run a knife along the sides of the pans, then flip them out onto the cooling rack. Peel off the parchment and allow to cool completely before frosting with Coconut Faux Cream Cheese Frosting (see page 140).

Coconut Faux Cream Cheese Frosting

To match the flavor of a classic cream cheese icing without using cheese was a challenge. You need that sour/tart flavor with that unmistakeably "cheesy" tang. Blending soaked cashews with various fats, a touch of sweetness, and some lemon and apple cider vinegar gives a pretty good copycat. This frosting is perfect for carrot cakes, red velvet cakes, cupcakes, fillings, and as a topping for brownies and other bars.

YIELD: 3 CUPS

1 cup raw cashews, soaked 4–24 hours

1 cup coconut oil, room temperature

½ cup coconut butter (aka manna or
    creamed coconut)

¼ cup palm oil shortening, room temperature

½ cup pastured butter, room temperature
    (or use additional palm oil shortening in
    same quantity)

Juice of ½ lemon, approximately 3 tbsp

¼ cup maple syrup

2 tsp pure vanilla extract

2 tbsp apple cider vinegar

½ tsp sea salt

1. Drain the cashews. In a blender or food processor, blend the soaked cashews until as smooth as possible.

2. Add the remaining ingredients and process until smooth and completely blended.

3. Frost your cake! Start by placing the first layer on a cake stand or flat plate. Pile about 1 cup (or one third of the recipe) into the middle, smoothing out to within ½ inch of the edges. Stack on the second cake layer. Put another ½ cup onto the top and spread a very thin layer of frosting all over the cake. This is the crumb coat and keeps stray crumbs from ruining the perfection of the white frosting. Then spread on the rest of the frosting. Keep cake refrigerated for a hard frosting or at room temperature for a softer texture.

Chocolate-Avocado Mousse

At first glance, this dessert sounds like a mistake; chocolate and avocado, together? But fear not. Even if you don't like avocado, the remaining ingredients in this dessert meld beautifully to create a wonderfully rich, smooth, and decadent dessert. The avocado adds a creaminess and richness that is mellow enough to marry up with the chocolate, coffee, and a touch of sweetness from the maple syrup. Make this a few hours in advance to allow the mousse to harden up a bit or eat it straight out of the blender or food processor for a warm custard-like treat.

YIELD: 4–6 SERVINGS

3 tbsp coconut oil

1 oz 100 percent pure dark chocolate

3 tbsp cacao powder

1 tsp instant coffee granules

6 pitted medjool dates (as soft as possible)

2 large ripe avocados, pitted

¼ cup full-fat coconut milk

2 tbsp maple syrup

1 tsp pure vanilla extract

1. Set a small metal bowl atop a small saucepan of water, filled about one third of the way. Set on high heat until it boils, then turn down to a simmer.

2. Melt the coconut oil, chocolate, cacao powder, and coffee in the bowl, stirring occasionally. Set aside while preparing the next part of the recipe.

3. In a blender or food processor, combine the remaining ingredients and blend until almost smooth.

4. Add the chocolate mixture and continue to blend until completely smooth.

5. Scoop or pipe into glass bowls. Place in refrigerator to firm up for 4 hours or eat it soft and warm straight out of the blender.

Dark Chocolate Cherry Muffins

My kids like to take easy-to-handle snacks to school with them, but many schools these days have no-nut regulations. When you are gluten/grain-free, this can pose some serious challenges to the lunch box conundrum. Luckily these muffins contain no nuts or nut products and are completely safe for most schools. Keep them refrigerated in a covered container for up to three days, although in my house, they rarely last two.

YIELD: 12 MUFFINS

¾ cup coconut flour, sifted if lumpy

¼ cup arrowroot flour

½ tsp sea salt

½ tsp baking soda

⅓ cup cocoa powder

6 eggs

½ cup maple syrup or honey (or for even lower
     sugar content use ⅓ cup maple syrup or honey
     and ½ tsp liquid stevia)

⅓ cup coconut or almond milk

2 tsp pure vanilla extract

½ cup coconut oil, melted

1 tbsp apple cider vinegar

¾ cup frozen pitted dark sweet cherries, chopped
     (about 1½ cups when whole)

1. Preheat oven to 350°F. Line a muffin pan with paper cups or grease well with coconut oil.

2. In a large bowl, sift together the flours, salt, baking soda, and cocoa. Stir to combine and set aside.

3. In a separate bowl, combine the wet ingredients (except the cherries) and whisk to blend evenly.

4. Pour the wet into the dry and whisk until completely mixed. Allow to sit for 1 to 2 minutes to let the coconut flour thicken.

5. Stir in the cherries.

6. Pour evenly into the lined or greased muffin pan and bake for 25 to 30 minutes. Muffins are done when a toothpick inserted into the middle of the muffins comes out clean.

7. Cool on a wire rack for 10 to 15 in muffin pan. Remove muffins from pan and allow to cool completely on wire rack before storing.

High-Protein Lemon-Coconut–Poppy Seed Muffins

Muffins are one of my favorite snack foods to make. They can be loaded up with plenty of goodness in a tiny little package and they can be easily packed into bags and lunch boxes. The flavor of a Meyer lemon is a bit different than a regular lemon and can only be described as more floral. If you can't find Meyer lemons (they can be hard to find out of season), regular old lemons will do just fine.

YIELD: 12 MUFFINS

¾ cup coconut flour, sifted if lumpy

½ tsp sea salt

2 tsp baking powder

¼ cup poppy seeds

¼ cup cacao nibs or mini chocolate chips, optional

7 eggs

Zest and juice of 1 Meyer lemon

⅓ cup coconut oil, melted

¼ cup maple syrup or honey

2 tsp vanilla extract

½ cup coconut cream (see note)

Shredded coconut to garnish (optional)

Note: Coconut cream can be purchased in some health food stores, or alternatively you can place a can of coconut milk in the fridge upside down overnight. The next morning, open the top, pour off the water, and use what's left in smoothies and this recipe!

1. Preheat oven to 350°F. Grease or line a 12-muffin tin.

2. In a large bowl, mix all the dry ingredients together.

3. In a separate bowl, mix the wet ingredients together.

4. Pour the dry ingredients into the wet and stir to combine.

5. Evenly portion out the batter into muffin tin and bake for 20 minutes.

6. Remove from oven and cool on cooling rack for 10 minutes. Remove muffins from tin and continue to cool on cooling rack. Store in airtight container for up to 3 days.

Blueberry Muffins

These muffins are a great way to use up fresh summer fruits and go well with pretty much any flavor. You can even use chocolate chips instead of fruit (just reduce to ½ cup). Raspberries, blackberries, blueberries, chopped strawberries—they all stand up to the thick batter. When storing, keep in a sealed container in the refrigerator and consume within four or five days. They freeze quite well and make great snacks. Simply remove from the freezer in the morning and by lunchtime they are perfectly defrosted.

YIELD: 12 MUFFINS

¾ cup coconut flour, sifted if lumpy

Rounded ¼ tsp sea salt

Rounded ¼ tsp baking soda

¼ tsp ground cinnamon

Dash of ground nutmeg

6 pastured eggs

⅓ cup maple syrup

2 full droppers of liquid stevia

⅓ cup whole-milk yogurt (grass-fed if possible)

1 tbsp pure vanilla extract

⅓ cup + 3 tbsp coconut oil, melted

1 cup wild blueberries (frozen berries work
     very well too)

1. Preheat the oven to 350°F. Grease or line your muffin tins with paper (or use a silicone muffin pan).

2. In a small bowl, stir the dry ingredients together.

3. Add all the wet ingredients to the bowl with the dry ingredients and then stir together with a fork, whisk, or small handheld stick blender. All methods will work, just make sure to get the lumps out.

4. Spoon into muffin tins until almost full (these rise to a fraction of the size of a traditional muffin). Place in preheated oven and bake for 25 to 30 minutes.

5. Muffins are done when just golden brown on edges and a toothpick inserted comes out clean.

6. Remove to a cooling rack and cool for 10 minutes. Remove from tins and allow to cool completely.

Vanilla-Bean Ice Cream

There are plenty of options out there for non-dairy versions of our favorite childhood treat, ice cream, but none comes close to the creaminess found in this rich, decadent coconut oil version. With the addition of coconut cream and coconut oil, this ice cream is smooth, rich, and thick. It is best served the day you make it, but if there are leftovers (which is rare around our house), simply remove the ice cream from the freezer twenty to thirty minutes prior to serving for best results.

YIELD: 6–8 SERVINGS

½ cup coconut oil

1 vanilla bean, scraped of its seeds

½ cup maple syrup

½ tsp sea salt

8 pastured egg yolks

1 tbsp pure vanilla extract

1 (14-oz) can full-fat coconut milk (can should read 53–55 percent coconut extract)

1 (14-oz) can coconut cream (70 percent or higher coconut extract; see note)

Note: Coconut cream can also be made by refrigerating a can of coconut milk for 4 hours or more, then flipping it over, removing the lid, and pouring off the water. You will need to use 2 cans of coconut milk to get the required 14 oz of coconut cream.

1. In a small saucepan over medium heat, melt the coconut oil. Remove from the heat, add in the vanilla bean seeds and pod (it will be removed in a later step), cover, and allow to sit at room temperature for 20 to 30 minutes or up to a few hours if needed.

2. Remove the vanilla bean pod from the pan, add in the maple syrup, salt, egg yolks, and vanilla extract and blend with an immersion blender or in a countertop blender until smooth.

3. Pour in the coconut milk and cream, blend again, and return to saucepan.

4. Turn the heat to medium and grab a whisk. Whisk the custard constantly. When it comes to a boil, turn it down to a simmer, continuing to whisk, until it begins to thicken. Allow to simmer 8 to 10 minutes. The custard should be thick enough that if you dip in a wooden spoon, take it out, and drag your finger across the back, the custard will not run back together but will instead stay in place. That is a nice, thick custard.

5. Pour the custard into a metal bowl, cover with plastic wrap (leaving a corner propped open so the heat can escape), and place it in the fridge to cool for 2 to 3 hours. Stir every 30 minutes for the first hour to avoid a skin on top.

6. When it's cool enough, put it into your ice-cream maker and follow the manufacturer's instructions. Once it has reached a soft-serve consistency, put it in the freezer for 2 to 3 hours to firm up.

7. Serve with Grilled Pineapples (see page 153).

GRILLED PINEAPPLES

Grilling fruit brings out an even more tongue-tingling sweetness than letting it ripen to perfection. The natural sugars contained in most fruit caramelizes beautifully when grilled (think peaches, figs, or strawberries). Grilled fruits make a perfect accompaniment for creamy ice creams, yogurts, and dips or even as a complement to rich grilled meats like steaks or chops. Chop up for salads (fruit or green) or eat straight off the grill. The possibilities are endless.

YIELD: 4–6 SERVINGS

1 tbsp honey

2 tbsp coconut oil, melted

1 ripe pineapple, peeled, cored, and sliced into rings

1. Mix honey and coconut oil together. Brush over pineapple rings.

2. On an outdoor grill or barbecue, set temperature to medium high.

3. Grill pineapple rings until golden brown, remove from heat, and eat right off the grill or slice into bite-size pieces and cool to room temperature. Serve over ice cream (see page 150) or yogurt.

Dark Chocolate Ice Cream

Dark chocolate is my vice. I'll tell you a secret: I eat a piece almost every night. The darker the better! I could happily be on a dessert, I mean desert, island and have nothing but chocolate and coconuts to feed me and I would be one happy lady. This recipe makes an exceptionally thick custard. If you find it is too thick for your ice-cream maker, simply pop it in the freezer in a large container, stir every 30 minutes or so for a couple of hours, and you'll have perfectly scoopable ice cream in no time.

YIELD: 4 CUPS OR 2 PINTS

½ cup coconut oil

½ cup maple syrup

½ tsp sea salt

8 pastured egg yolks

½ cup cocoa powder

1 tbsp pure vanilla extract

1 (14-oz) can full-fat coconut milk (can should read 53–55 percent coconut extract)

1 (14-oz) can coconut cream (70 percent or higher coconut extract; see note)

Note: Coconut cream can also be made by refrigerating a can of coconut milk for 4 hours or more, then flipping it over, removing the lid, and pouring off the water. You will need to use 2 cans of coconut milk to get the required 14 oz of coconut cream.

1. In a medium saucepan, melt the coconut oil over medium heat.

2. Using an immersion blender, blend in the remaining ingredients. Set over medium heat and cook, whisking constantly, until very thick (about 10 minutes).

3. Pour into a metal bowl and cool, semi-covered (to allow heat to escape) in the refrigerator for 3 to 4 hours or until completely cold throughout.

4. Pour into your ice-cream maker and follow the manufacturer's instructions. Scrape into a container and freeze for 3 to 4 hours for best texture.

Chocolate, Avocado, Coconut, and Lime Pie

This pie is green. Some people don't like that. Let me tell you this: They haven't tasted this pie. Yes, the pie's main ingredient is avocado, but the lime, vanilla, and coconut oil cut the flavor quite beautifully. The chocolate layer is a bit of a bonus but makes for an interesting texture amongst the softer crust and pudding-like filling. If there are leftovers, the top layer of avocado might discolor a small amount to a browner shade of green, but not to worry . . . it will still taste fantastic. Make sure to cover tightly and consume within two to three days.

YIELD: 1 (9-INCH) PIE

For the Crust

1½ cups unsweetened coconut chips

½ cup blanched almond meal

Juice and zest of 1 lime

¼ tsp sea salt

1 cup medjool dates, pitted

2 tsp pure vanilla extract

¼ cup coconut oil, melted

For the Chocolate Layer

3 oz unsweetened chocolate

2 tbsp coconut oil

1 tbsp maple syrup (optional)

For the Filling

3 large, ripe avocados (about 2 cups)

Juice and zest of 2 limes

⅓ cup maple syrup or honey

¼ cup coconut oil, melted

¼ tsp sea salt

1 tsp pure vanilla extract

1. Prepare the crust: In a food processor or heavy-duty blender, blend all crust ingredients until well blended but a little chunky. Pat into a greased 9-inch glass pie plate. Chill in freezer while moving to the next step.

2. Make the chocolate layer: In a double-boiler or a metal bowl resting over a pot of simmering water, melt the chocolate and coconut oil together. Add maple syrup if you think you might not like the deep, rich flavor of unsweetened chocolate.

3. Pour the chocolate over the cooled crust and swirl it around to cover all the surface area. Put it back in the freezer to cool completely.

4. Make the filling: In a blender, blend all filling ingredients until smooth. Pour over solidified chocolate layer and chill for 4 to 6 hours.

5. Serve with whipped coconut cream if desired.

Chocolate-Strawberry Icebox Pie

Icebox pies are a great way to make a cheesecake-type pie without using any cream cheese or any other dairy for that matter. The cashews in this recipe act like the cheese and create a sturdy layer of delicious filling that holds up well even when defrosted. Chocolate and strawberries marry together in this icebox pie to create a classic pairing of flavors. If you serve the pie with sliced strawberries on top and have leftovers, just remember that the strawberries will freeze solid and will be difficult to eat unless fully defrosted.

YIELD: 1 (9-INCH) PIE

For the Crust

1½ cups almond meal

½ cup cocoa powder

½ tsp sea salt

2 tbsp coconut oil

½ cup pitted medjool dates (8–9 dates)

2 tsp pure vanilla extract

1 pastured egg

For the Filling

2 cups raw cashews, soaked in filtered water overnight

½ cup coconut butter, softened

½ cup coconut oil, softened

¼ cup honey

1 vanilla bean, scraped of its seeds

2 tsp pure vanilla extract

½ cup fresh strawberries, pureed

Juice of 1 lime

Zest of ½ lime

1. Prepare the crust: Preheat oven to 350°F. In a small bowl, stir together the almond meal, cocoa powder, and sea salt. Set aside.

2. In the bowl of a food processor, pulse the coconut oil, dates, vanilla, and egg until liquid. Add the cocoa-almond meal and mix until combined.

3. Grease a 9-inch glass pie plate and rub some coconut oil onto your hands as well. Pour the crust mixture into the pie plate and pat it evenly all around the bottom and sides. Bake in preheated oven for 12 to 15 minutes. Remove and cool completely.

4. Make the filling: Drain cashews. Place cashews, coconut butter, coconut oil, honey, vanilla bean seeds, vanilla extract, strawberry puree, lime juice, and zest into the bowl of a food processor. Blend until completely smooth and liquefied.

5. Pour over crust, smooth out with spatula, and freeze for at least 4 hours. Defrost for 30 minutes prior to serving.

Pear Tart

Pie making without gluten can be more frustrating than weeding an organic garden in the peak of summer, but in the absence of grains it can be even more difficult. This crust is carefully concocted to be as similar to a lard-and-flour crust as possible. It is crisp after baking and has just the right bite to it. Replace the pear with apple for a good old-fashioned home-style apple pie, or even fresh summer berries when they are in abundance.

YIELD: 1 (9-INCH) PIE

For the Crust

¾ cup coconut flour

½ cup raw cashews, finely ground

2 tbsp coconut palm sugar

¼ tsp sea salt

¼ cup coconut oil, room temperature

¼ cup coconut cream, softened but not melted

3 pastured eggs, beaten

1 tsp pure vanilla extract

For the Filling

1½–2 pounds Bartlett pears (about 8 medium pears)

Juice and zest of 1 Meyer lemon

¼ tsp sea salt

¼ tsp ground ginger

1 tsp pure vanilla extract

1 tbsp tapioca starch

½ tsp cinnamon

1. Prepare the crust: Mix the flour, cashews, sugar, and salt together in a small bowl until well combined. With a fork, mash in the coconut oil, coconut cream, eggs, and vanilla. Once a dough is formed, set aside.

2. Grease a 9-inch tart pan or glass pie dish. Put the dough into the dish and press into the bottom and up the sides. Try to get it as even as possible. Chill for at least 1 hour in the fridge while you make the filling.

3. Make the filling: Peel, core, and slice the pears. In a large bowl, mix the pears with the remaining ingredients.

4. Preheat the oven to 450°F. Pour the filling into the crust and place in the oven for 15 minutes. Reduce the temperature to 350°F for 25 to 35 minutes. Remove from oven and cool on a wire rack. Best served at room temperature. To store, keep in the fridge and remove 30 minutes prior to serving.

Lemon Meringue Pie

My father has a taste for lemon meringue pie and when I asked him what he wanted for Father's Day, he said, "Lemon meringue pie!" How could I pass up the challenge? The key to this pie is to eat it all as fast as you can. The maple syrup in the egg whites has a tendency to cause weeping faster than a regular meringue pie. Though I've heard that meringue should never go in the fridge, this pie does fine when refrigerated. Weeping will occur almost as soon as it is out of the oven, but it keeps for up to two days on the counter, covered, at room temperature.

YIELD: 1 (9-INCH) PIE

For the Crust

½ cup coconut flour, sifted if lumpy

1 cup almond meal or flour

¼ cup tapioca or arrowroot flour

½ tsp sea salt

⅓ cup coconut oil, room temperature (soft)

2 pastured eggs

2 tbsp maple syrup

1 tsp pure vanilla extract

For the Filling

6 pastured eggs

½ cup lemon juice (approximately 3–4 lemons)

3 tbsp maple syrup

½ cup coconut butter

½ cup coconut oil, very cold and cut into pieces (keep cold until needed)

2 tbsp lemon zest (approximately 3 lemons)

For the Meringue

4 pastured egg whites

3 tbsp maple syrup or honey

½ tsp cream of tartar

1. Prepare the crust: Preheat oven to 350°F. In a large bowl, mix together the flours and sea salt. Mash in the oil with a fork.

2. In a separate, smaller bowl, whisk the eggs with the syrup and vanilla. Pour into the flour mixture and form into a dough.

3. Press into a 9-inch tart pan or greased glass pie plate, right up the sides. Poke all around the crust to make sure it doesn't bubble up during baking. Blind bake (bake without a filling) the crust for 10 to 12 minutes. Remove from oven and cool at room temperature.

4. Make the filling: Preheat the oven to 350°F. Fill a medium pot one third of the way with water. Set on stove over high heat and bring to a boil. Lower to a simmer.

5. In a large metal bowl, whisk the eggs, lemon juice, and maple syrup. Place over the simmering water and whisk constantly until very thick, about 10 minutes. Add in the coconut butter and allow to melt, stirring to combine.

6. Remove from the heat and put in the cold coconut oil pieces a few at a time, whisking between additions. Add the lemon zest and stir.

7. Pour over the cooled crust and bake in preheated oven for 10 minutes.

8. Make the meringue: In a large metal bowl, using a handheld beater or immersion blender with whisk attachment, blend the egg whites and maple syrup or honey until foamy. Add the cream of tartar and beat on high until soft peaks form. (This may take longer than usual because of the extra liquid, but it will happen, just be patient!)

9. Pour meringue over the tart and bake again in the 350°F oven for 10 to 15 minutes. Remove from oven and cool to room temperature before serving.

Maple-Bacon-Chocolate Chip Cookies

The bacon craze that has washed over the Internet for the past few years has been something of a savior for good-quality, thick-cut bacon. I prefer to get mine from a local butcher where I know I can find humane, pastured pork that has been cured in-house with only the finest ingredients. Don't skimp on the quality of the bacon in this recipe; it really is the star of the show. You may wonder why I, or anyone for that matter, would put bacon in a cookie, but you'll wonder no more after you try these. Though they aren't your average crunchy on the outside, soft on the inside cookies, these babies shine in their own light with crunchy bacon and a pillowy soft cookie surrounding it.

YIELD: 12 COOKIES

For the Candied Bacon

8 slices thick-cut bacon

3–4 tbsp maple syrup

For the Cookie Dough

⅔ cup coconut flour, sifted if lumpy

⅓ cup arrowroot flour

½ tsp sea salt

½ tsp baking powder

½ tsp baking soda

⅓ cup coconut oil

¼ cup coconut sugar

¼ cup coconut butter

¼ cup honey

3 pastured eggs

2 tsp pure vanilla extract

½ tsp apple cider vinegar

¼ cup dark chocolate chips or chunks

1. Prepare the candied bacon: Preheat the oven to 275°F. Lay the bacon on a wire rack set over a baking tray (alternatively, you can lay the bacon directly on the tray, but the rack gives a crispier finish to the bacon). Brush the maple syrup onto the bacon, flip it, and repeat on the other side. Bake for 60 to 90 minutes, checking often. Baking times vary greatly depending on the thickness of the bacon, so check to make sure it's not cooking too fast. When it's a deep golden color, remove it from the oven and cool on the rack until needed (if you used a tray, remove it immediately to a wire rack to cool; otherwise it will get stuck to the tray). The bacon will crisp up once it begins to cool.

2. Make the cookie dough: Turn the oven up to 350°F. In a large bowl, mix the flours, salt, baking powder, and baking soda.

3. In a separate bowl, cream the coconut oil and coconut sugar together. Add in the coconut butter and honey and cream again.

4. Add eggs, one at a time, mixing thoroughly between additions. Stir in the vanilla and apple cider vinegar.

5. Chop or crumble the bacon into the batter, then stir in the chocolate chips.

6. Combine the wet and dry ingredients, scoop out onto cookie sheets, and flatten slightly with a fork or your hand.

7. Bake for 12 to 15 minutes. Remove from oven and cool 10 minutes on cookie sheet. Remove to wire racks to cool completely.

Dark Chocolate-Coconut-Orange Truffles

Truffles are a must for dark chocolate lovers everywhere. They are simple to make, easy to hold, great for parties, they melt in your mouth, and they are full of the many health benefits of coconut oil and the abundant antioxidants of dark chocolate. These truffles are also free of dairy and refined sugar. They keep very well in the refrigerator, but because of the nature of coconut oil and its tendency to harden under cold conditions, remove the truffles from the fridge at least 20 minutes prior to serving. Do not keep at room temperature.

YIELD: 24 TRUFFLES

2 oz pure cacao butter

3 tbsp honey

¼ cup coconut oil

Zest of 1 navel orange

1 tbsp pure vanilla extract

7 oz (200 g) 90 to 100 percent dark chocolate,
    broken into chunks

¼ cup coconut butter, melted

3 tbsp coconut milk

¼ cup cocoa powder

Cocoa powder for dusting (optional)

Shredded coconut for rolling (optional)

1. In a double-boiler, a metal bowl over boiling water (don't let bowl touch the water), or the microwave, melt cacao butter.

2. Stir in the honey, followed by the coconut oil, orange zest, and vanilla.

3. Add the dark chocolate chunks and the coconut butter, and stir until combined.

4. Remove the saucepan from the heat. Whisk in the coconut milk and cocoa powder. Pour into a glass dish and set in the refrigerator for 2 to 4 hours. You want the consistency to be that of fudge, but not too hard.

5. Remove from the fridge and allow to stand at room temperature until it is soft enough to roll.

6. Scoop using small spoons or a melon baller, roll with your hands (you're going to get dirty!) into balls, and either set on a cookie sheet to be placed back in the fridge or roll in the shredded coconut and cocoa powder first. Refrigerate the finished balls until serving.

Chocolate Peppermint Patties

Although I'm not a huge fan of peppermint and chocolate mixed together, once I mixed real peppermint into this recipe, I was hooked. Fresh peppermint is something altogether different than the extracts you can buy in the store. If you must use extract, try to find pure peppermint oil in the food section of your health store. The flavor is refreshing and the patties just melt in your mouth (and in your hand!).

YIELD: 20–24 PATTIES

½ cup coconut butter, softened but not liquid

3 tbsp honey

2 tsp pure vanilla extract

½ cup fresh mint leaves or ½ tsp pure peppermint
   oil or extract

¾ cup coconut oil

¼ cup coconut milk

100g (3½ oz) 90 to 100 percent dark chocolate

1. Mash the coconut butter with the honey and vanilla. Set aside.

2. In a small saucepan, muddle the mint by either mashing it with a kitchen utensil or squishing it in the palm of your hand. You just want to release the essential oils. Add the coconut oil to the mint and melt it over low heat. Remove from the heat and allow mint to sit in the oil for at least 15 minutes. Strain out the mint and mix the coconut milk into the oil with a whisk. Pour into the coconut butter mixture and stir to combine.

3. Cool for 1 to 2 hours and mash to blend it (if it has separated). Bring it up to room temperature for the next step.

4. Line a baking tray with parchment paper. Scoop out small balls of the mixture and form into little patties. Place on the baking tray and continue until all the batter is in patties on the tray. Place in freezer for at least 20 minutes to harden. While you're waiting, melt the chocolate.

5. In a double-boiler or a small metal bowl placed over a small pot of gently simmering water, add the chocolate and melt completely. Dip each hardened patty into the chocolate, rolling to coat (move quickly to avoid melting), and lay back on the tray. Continue until all patties are coated. Cool in refrigerator until hardened.

6. Keep stored in refrigerator for up to 7 days.

Roasted Banana Bread

When I was a kid learning to cook and bake, one of my favorite things to make was banana bread. I had an old recipe from *America Cooks* that called for a cup of sour cream. It was amazing, dense, chock-full of greasy goodness, and it filled you right up after one slice. When I switched to grain-free, one of the first things I experimented with was loaves of quick breads. Somewhat easier on the novice baker because they don't need to rise to make a perfect loaf, quick breads are perfect for baking with your kids. This version is my absolute favorite because when you roast the bananas, it caramelizes them and the flavor is outstanding.

YIELD: 1 LOAF

3 medium bananas (about 1½ cups)

⅔ cup coconut flour, sifted if lumpy

½ cup arrowroot flour

1 tsp ground cinnamon

¼ tsp ground cardamom

¼ tsp ground nutmeg

1 tsp baking soda

1 tsp baking powder

½ tsp sea salt

⅓ cup coconut oil

4 pastured eggs, separated

2 tsp pure vanilla extract

¼ cup honey

1 tsp liquid stevia

¼ cup coconut milk

(½ tsp cream of tartar)

1. Preheat oven to 400°F and grease a 4 x 8-inch loaf pan.

2. Lay bananas on a baking tray (unpeeled) and roast for 15 minutes. Remove and cool to room temperature. Turn oven down to 350°F.

3. Sift dry ingredients into a large bowl. Set aside.

4. Peel the cooled bananas, and mash them in a separate large bowl. Add the coconut oil, egg yolks, vanilla extract, honey, stevia, and coconut milk and whisk until blended. Set aside.

5. In a large metal bowl beat the egg whites until foamy. Add the cream of tartar and beat again until stiff peaks form.

6. Add the wet ingredients to the dry and mix completely. Fold in the egg whites with a spatula and pour into the greased loaf pan. Bake for 45 to 55 minutes. Remove from oven and cool in pan for 20 minutes. Remove from pan and cool completely on baking rack.

- didn't separate eggs
- good texture - more on dry side

Sandwich Bread

My kids complained for months about not being able to have nut butter and jam sandwiches in their lunches after we went grain-free. After numerous failed attempts at a bread that could stand up to snacking, sandwiches, or toasting, I finally figured it out. The texture of this bread is perfect for anything you would normally make with regular wheat bread. It's a bit plain to eat on its own but stands up well to everything we've thrown at it so far. If you've been hankering for a BLT or a croque monsieur since you went grain-free, it's time to welcome back an old friend.

YIELD: 1 SMALL LOAF

¾ cup almond butter, smooth

6 pastured eggs

2 tbsp honey

¼ cup coconut oil, melted

½ tsp apple cider vinegar

¼ cup golden flax, ground

3 tbsp coconut flour

1 tsp baking soda

½ tsp sea salt

1. Preheat oven to 350°F. Line a 4 x 8-inch loaf pan with parchment and grease well with coconut oil.

2. In a large bowl, blend the almond butter, eggs, honey, coconut oil, and apple cider vinegar with an immersion blender.

3. In a separate bowl, combine the flax, coconut flour, baking soda, and sea salt. Mix the dry into the wet, pour into the greased and lined loaf pan, and bake for 35 to 40 minutes.

PALEO TIPS

"Let food be thy medicine and medicine be thy food."

— Hippocrates

I've been asked a lot of questions from fans and readers who have been following me since before I went paleo, usually something along the lines of "What are the first steps to going paleo?" "What sites/resources do you recommend for going paleo?"

This info should help anyone who is thinking of going paleo find their way. These tips are short, concise, and will help you figure out what your first steps should be. Without further ado, I give you my Top 10 Tips for Going Paleo:

10. Start Small

If the thought of giving up processed foods, grains, dairy, sugar, legumes, and refined vegetable oils all at the same time scares you, start removing them one at a time. Start with the baby step of removing processed foods. Feel better without all the packaged, unpronounceable ingredients? Start removing grains next (thereby removing gluten, a big irritant for a lot of people). Remove each component for a minimum of one week before moving to the next one. You'll start to feel amazing after the first two weeks, I promise.

9. Commit and Plan

Get rid of all the non-paleo junk in your house that may tempt you as you slowly ease into the lifestyle. Look for hidden sugars, grains, unrecognizable ingredients, and especially refined oils. Donate unopened packages to food banks if you can, or to food drives at your children's school. I sometimes have a hard time donating food that I wouldn't eat myself, but I know most people aren't as critical of their food as I am, so donate away! Plan out your week of meals each Sunday so you can shop and prep in advance if you need to. Knowing what every meal will entail and what you'll need for packing lunches makes life a breeze compared to "winging it." Failing to plan means you are planning to fail.

8. Remember, This Is Not a "Diet"

Committing to the paleo diet means not considering it a "diet." If you are serious about it after the first experimental weeks, commit to it and welcome it as the way of life you plan on continuing for as long as it works for you. Looking at it as a diet is asking for failure. Don't look at foods as things you *can't* have but as things you *won't* or *shouldn't* have. Look at it as a choice you are making to feel and look better. Once you're in, paleo becomes a lifestyle. You see everything as being "paleo," from foods to hair products to the way you renovate your house. The word *paleo* is merely a way for people in the community to recognize others of the same mindset. For most of us, it is less about what our ancestors ate and more a way to eat better, live better, and be better. Paleo is a movement.

7. Transition Your Kids as Slowly as You Are and They Might Not Even Notice

Kids want to eat what they have access to. As a parent, you can steer your child in any direction right from his or her first meal. Will it be mushy rice-based cereal or will it be a fresh, ripe, and gorgeously green avocado? My kids each started differently, one the normal cereal-based route but with all homemade baby foods and breastmilk until 22 months, while the other started on organic veggies and avocado plus breastmilk. They both LOVE

eating paleo and will go so far as to ask if something they are about to eat has gluten or sugar in it. That being said, they have a lot of wiggle room in their diets as we don't want to be too restrictive or pushy. We give them the guidelines and only offer paleo foods at home (with the occasional treat) and they know when they are out at school, parties, or relatives' houses that they can eat what is offered (within reason). They have never complained and see paleo as their normal.

6. Get Recipes from Blogs

Blogs, recipe sites, online booksellers, bookstores, friends—all these places offer recipes, tips, guidelines, advice, and more on the lifestyle and the various offshoots of it. Blogs like mine are filled to the brim with free recipes and advice, and they are all over the Internet. A lot of the top paleo blogs will link to other top paleo blogs, which can lead you to the best of the very best in terms of recipes, advice, and more. See my resources list for some suggestions.

5. Stock Up

Keep your house stocked with paleo foods for your fridge, freezer, and pantry and cook more than you need for a meal so that you always have something quick to eat that isn't processed foods or nuts. Nuts are great but they should not be a regular snack as they contain as much or more phytic acid as grains and they are extremely calorie dense, making them a poor choice for people looking to stay slim or achieve a healthy weight. Keep fruit, coconut, dried meat, cut vegetables, hard boiled eggs, olives, leftover meals, etc., in the fridge for easy pickins. Buy large quantities of fruits and vegetables when they are on sale. Dry, vacuum seal, freeze, or can to keep produce fresh as long as possible. Make sure there is always something at hand for kids and adults alike or you'll be scrambling for something quick and easy or skipping meals, neither of which is a good option.

4. Make Friends in the Paleo Community

Find people who eat like you do. Tell everyone you are going paleo and see what other people are saying. As soon as we went paleo, so did a good portion of our families and friends, or they at least gave it a try. Doing it with other people is the safest way to go. Not only can you support each other with your choices or when you are feeling like giving up, but you can also share awesome resources you've discovered in your community and even have dinner together once or twice a month to really share that community spirit. There's just something special about sharing this lifestyle, and it's amazing when you all feel great about your food choices together.

3. Eat Non-Paleo at Least Once a Week

Although paleo is a great way to eat, it's also fun to have a treat here and there. There is a lot of disagreement within the community about what constitutes a paleo "cheat," but I think it's something each person has to decide for him- or herself. I feel terribly when I eat gluten, so I just avoid it altogether. If I'm going to a movie, do I skip the giant bag of buttery popcorn? Hell no, that's a treat. At Christmas, there will be chocolate and lots of it. Some of our friends go all out, hamburgers with buns, real cake made with flour. Judge not, lest ye be judged, I say... Experiment: have some sugar, or pastured heavy cream, or cake, or popcorn, or grass-fed butter or whey protein after exercising. Do what makes you happy and then forget about it. Do NOT feel guilty when you cheat. There is no wagon, you haven't stepped off of it when you eat something non-paleo and you shouldn't punish yourself with excessive exercise. Feel good about the other 90 percent of the time and feel good when you cheat that 10 percent of the time (or 20 percent...).

2. Make Farmers Your Friends

Go in on a quarter of a cow, pig, or lamb, or buy chickens in bulk from your local farmers. Get to know them, introduce yourself, visit their land and see what the animals do all day. Ask about what the animals eat—GMO or non-GMO feed? Are they pastured, free-range, organic? How much do you have to buy to get the lowest price? Is cutting, wrapping, and delivery all included? Were the animals "finished" on something other than their normal fare? Are hormones or antibiotics used and, if so, what are the farm's policies regarding them? How far in advance do you need to order? Do they operate all year long or are they small scale (usually selling only in spring and fall)? Then ask yourself some questions: Can four of your friends go in on a cow together? Do you have enough freezer space? These are all very important questions to ask. Go to farmers' markets, ask questions at local butcher shops and retail stores. Find Facebook pages and like them. Get yourself into your local food scene.

1. Personalize

Not everyone can eat a strict paleo diet. Some do low carb, some do autoimmune, some cheat with gluten-filled pastries, some won't touch the stuff even on cheat days. Some can eat like a horse and not gain weight, and some start packing on the pounds with all the dense foods. After the initial 30 to 90 days of eating paleo, start adding foods back in to see if you tolerate them. If you tolerate dairy, add some back in. If you tolerate legumes, have hummus once in a while. Do what works for you, but just stick to the main principles for the majority of the time to reap the full benefits that paleo has to offer. A good rule of thumb is: 100 percent paleo, 80 percent of the time. Some things you can do to maximize your lifestyle: Add good quality Himalayan pink salt to your morning water; add supplements you think you might be missing (I take calcium,

magnesium, and Vitamin D); add protein shakes and extra carbohydrates if you work out heavily; research ways to make yourself feel as well as possible. Some of us have been eating such crap for so long we have no idea what it feels like to feel good.

So there it is in a nutshell. The paleo diet is fantastic and I will never eat any other way, it's really that good. It's not a fad, it's not a "Hollywood" diet, and it's not going anywhere. Do yourself a favor and try it out for a month to see the difference your food can make to your well-being.

Resources

There are many amazing sources of information on the ever-evolving nature of the Paleo diet out there. Here are a few of my favorites.

WEBSITES

http://marksdailyapple.com
http://robbwolf.com
http://chriskresser.com
http://paleoparents.com
http://theclothesmakethegirl.com
http://primalpalate.com

BOOKS

Against All Grain by Danielle Walker
Victory Belt Publishing, 2013

Everyday Paleo by Sarah Fragoso
Victory Belt Publishing, 2012

Gather, the Art of Paleo Entertaining by Bill Staley
    and Hayley Mason
Victory Belt Publishing, 2013

Make It Paleo by Bill Staley and Hayley Mason
Victory Belt Publishing, 2011

The Paleo Diet by Loren Cordain
Houghton Mifflin Harcourt, 2010

The Paleo Solution by Robb Wolf
Victory Belt Publishing, 2010

Practical Paleo by Diane Sanfilippo
Victory Belt Publishing, 2012

The Primal Blueprint by Mark Sisson
Primal Nutrition, Inc., 2012

Primal Cravings by Brandon and Megan Keatley
Primal Nutrition, Inc., 2013

Well Fed by Melissa Joulwan
Smudge Publishing, 2012

Index

Acknowledgments

With a special thank you to Alexis, Richard, and Alena, who supported me from the very beginning and always had my back. To Dirk and Judy for everything you've done to make our lives better and for your unconditional love. To Ian and Maren for being the best neighbors anyone could ask for and showing me that real work can be fun and functional, and to Zoe and Makena for telling me how it really is.

I would like to express my sincere gratitude to the many people who made this book possible. To Countryman Press for making my dreams come true. To my editor, Ann Treistman, for working with me in all aspects of this book—without your guidance I would surely have been lost along the way. To Christie, Dai, and Matt for helping with taste testing, recipe selection, and kick-assery. To Caitlin, Courtnee, and Joey for never leaving my side no matter what happens, even when I eat "weird," and finally, to all the people I've never met who read my words, acknowledged my sincerity, and joined in on the conversation to make this world a better, more healthful place.